Ask the Wine Guy

Designed by Marilyn Appleby Design
Edited by Roger Matuz

Library of Congress Catalog Card Number 2002 141267
ISBN 1-881892-06-9
Printed and bound in the United States of America.

Published by Spradlin & Associates,
PO Box 863, Lapeer, MI   48446. Telephone 810.664.8406.
First Edition.

RAPTOR PRESS

Raptor Press is an imprint of Spradlin & Associates.

Ask the Wine Guy

Everything You Always
Wanted to Know About Wine,
but Didn't Know Who to Ask

•

JOE BORRELLO

Contents

Enjoying Wine — Pure and Simple

After over twenty-five years of answering wine and food questions from friends, customers, radio listeners, readers and seminar participants, I have assembled a number of the most pertinent inquiries and responses in this book. The contents of these pages are not intended as a scholarly dissertation on wine. Although there is plenty of data, it is simply a collection of straightforward answers to questions frequently asked by curious and interested consumers.

Over the years I have accumulated this information from my own experiences in tasting, teaching and selling wine, through conversations with winemakers and friends in the trade and from reading a plethora of consumer and trade publications. Much of what you read in this book has been researched, remembered or otherwise assimilated from all these sources for which I am deeply indebted, but can no longer pinpoint the original source for literary credit. A significant amount of information has been transcribed from a vast number of notes on napkins, soaked-off wine labels, restaurant cash register receipts, matchbook covers, business cards, used envelopes, note pads and my personal writings. Also, in my research, I found two of the most useful and clear-cut sources of wine information for consumers and professionals alike were Leon D. Adams' *Commonsense Book of Wine* and Frank Schoonmacker's *Encyclopedia of Wine.* Both books approach the subject of wine in a sensible and uncomplicated manner.

Though I have addressed the questions with factual and practical answers, wine, like food, is a matter of personal taste, and there is no substitute for experience. I recommend finding a reputable merchant or asking a knowledgeable friend to guide you in trying various types of wines. Experiment with different wine and food tastes. Keep notes for future reference. You'll be amazed at how quickly you will accumulate knowledge of wine. The next best reference is to go right to the source — the winery. Visit those close to your home or check out wineries as you travel throughout this country and abroad. Ask questions and try various wine styles and varieties to find where your taste preferences lie and how they match with foods. For the finer points of wine, research the subject at your local library, on the Internet or join a wine and food group, such as Tasters Guild (www.tastersguild.com), and make new social contacts at the same time.

Not only will you broaden your knowledge about wine and food, but you will have fun doing it. But always remember, if *you* like a wine — by all means drink it and don't worry if it is politically or socially correct. Just enjoy!

Varieties & Styles

Wine…is one of the noblest
cordials in nature.

JOHN WESLEY

•

I never met a wine I didn't like.

JOE BORRELLO

Q: What is the most widely planted grape in the world? Cabernet Sauvignon, Chardonnay, or Zinfandel?

A: Oddly enough, it is none of the above. With over one million acres planted in Spain, the *Airén* grape claims the world title. *Airén* produces a rather undistinguished white wine, but it is used extensively to be distilled into brandy.

Q: Does varietal refer to the grape or the wine?

A: Varietal refers to wine that is made from at least 75% of one particular grape variety. Some typical examples of varietal wines are Cabernet Sauvignon, Merlot, Chardonnay, Pinot Noir, Riesling and many more. The tendency of late is to blend a mixture of compatible varieties in order to give the winemaker an opportunity to use the best grapes available and exercise some creative winemaking to produce the best possible product and value. These are called proprietary wines because they are a blend of wines developed by the proprietor and given creative label names that do not necessarily refer to the grape involved to make the wine. The premium Meritage and Rhone-style wines are popular proprietary wines that use classic French grape varieties in their blends.

Q: I am sometimes confused by all the talk of this grape or that, or this wine compared to that wine. Aren't all wines just fermented grape juice?

A: Yes, they are. Just like all cheeses are fermented milk. However, during the fermentation process many possible flavor combinations are introduced to the mix (through the use of yeast cultures, natural bacteria, production procedures, etc.) and the end products are distinctively different from each other. If you taste compare wines side by side you will easily recognize assorted fruit flavors from the various grape varieties. A good comparison is tasting a Granny Smith apple and a MacIntosh. They are both apples, but there are obvious variations in their flavors. The same applies to grape varieties. As the saying goes, "Experience is the best teacher." And there is no better way to train your taste buds and develop your palate than taste comparing wine varieties side by side.

Q: I have found quite a difference in dry wines. Are some less dry than others?

A: Winemakers will sometimes label their wines dry because they believe that their customers will not perceive the wine as sweet. Wines are chemically dry (the opposite of sweet) when there is no grape sugar left that could be fermented by yeast. From a sensory standpoint, wines are considered dry when any sweetness present is not perceived by the taster. Since the popular image of sweet wines is often limited to dessert wines, many people believe that they like dry wines when they actually prefer wines with some residual sugar. The taste threshold for sweetness generally falls between .5% and 1% residual sugar in wine. Since the word dry has no legal definition on a wine label, some wineries will label wines dry with as much as 2% sugar because they feel that is the level of sweetness the consumer favors or high acidity in the juice offsets higher sugar levels.

Q: Do all wines made with a particular grape, like Chardonnay, taste the same regardless of the winery brand?

A: Absolutely not. Regional weather and soil conditions have a profound effect on the taste of wine, and so do vineyard farming techniques and the winemaking style of the winemaker. All of these elements come into play in altering the taste of the final product. Higher vineyard yields have a tendency to water down the fullness of flavor in the grapes. The amount of residual sugar left in the juice after fermentation accounts for tastes that will range from dry to sweet, with many stages in between. The use, or lack of barrels in fermentation and aging the wine also has a tremendous effect on the final taste as directed by the winemaker. There are an infinite number of taste possibilities — all from the same grape.

Q: I do not like dry red wine. Is there any red wine not as sweet as Mogan David?

A: There are many regional wines in the United States that are a blend of grapes in various stages of sweetness. These are called proprietary wines and are usually excellent values. Visit some of your local winery tasting rooms or ask your wine merchant to guide you toward some semi-dry alternatives. Tasting different products is the only way you'll be able to determine your personal preferences in wine.

Q: Would you please explain the meaning of "foxy," "cloying" and "oxidized" in reference to tasting wine?

A: "Foxy" is the term used to describe the special taste quality of the native American grapes predominately found in the northeast and north central part of the United States. The best example of this taste is found in the Concord grape of the species *vitis labrusca.* Wines made from these grapes have a very pronounced aroma and taste, which is usually sweet. Grapes that have this characteristic foxy taste do not make particularly good wine, but do produce delicious juice, soda and jellies. "Cloying" describes a wine that has too much sweetness and too little acidity. "Oxidized" refers to a wine that has lost its freshness from too much contact with oxygen.

Q: I have really taken a liking to Merlot as my regular dinner red wine. Is this a fairly new variety?

A: The wine grape variety called Merlot has been around for some time. In France and California it was originally used as a blending grape for Cabernet Sauvignon and Cabernet Franc. The lighter style of the grape helps soften some of the harsh tannins found in the Cabernet grape wines. Over the last decade, Merlot has developed into one of the industry's fastest growing grape varieties, thanks in part to the expansion of Merlot as a wine variety on its own by California wineries. Because of the wine's early development and soft flavor, you and many other Americans have developed a fondness for this very food-compatible red wine. As a sidenote, although Merlot is currently a favorite wine variety, the "darling of the trade" in 1949 was Muscatel and the number one fruit crop in Napa Valley was prunes: how far we have come!

Q: I found a rather inexpensive bottle of French wine in the supermarket labeled *vin ordinaire.* Am I correct in assuming I did not find an overlooked treasure?

A: You do not have to have much knowledge of foreign languages to determine *vin ordinaire* translates to ordinary wine. Italy's *vino da tavola* and Germany's *tafelwein* also refer to common table wines that are consumed by most of the population in their respective countries.

Q: What is meant by the term "jug" wine?

A: "Jug" wines get their name from their large bottle size. Usually, bulk wines that are blended together to create a pleasant, inexpensive table wine for daily use are bottled in 1.5 or 3 to 5-liter jugs for convenience and volume usage. These are similar to the *vin ordinaire* (France), *vino da tavola* (Italy) or *tafelwein* (Germany). They are ordinary table wines of Europe that are value-oriented and are what people drink everyday. In the United States, these wines sometimes offer the best value in the marketplace. Many wine professionals consider American "jug" wines the best of this class in the world. United States technology has allowed our winemakers to produce large quantities of good quality wine, from premium grapes, with great consistency.

Q: How many different grapes varieties are there in the world?

A: A rough estimate would be over 5,000, and half of them are in Italy alone.

Q: Why do I like some Chardonnay wines and not others?

A: Chardonnay is historically the premier grape of the great white wines of Burgundy. In the last few decades this grape variety has also become the mainstay of the California wine trade, and, in most recent years, Chile and Australia. In all cases, Americans have a love affair with the wines made of Chardonnay grapes. However, the winemaking style can vary dramatically based on where the grapes are grown and how the juice is handled by the winemaker. In California, the grape has the ability to reach a heightened ripeness, unlike the cooler hillside vineyards of Burgundy. With the addition of oak barrels for fermentation and aging, the Californian Chardonnay produces a wine that is vanilla-scented and of rich texture. Classic Burgundian complexity utilizes the skillful mixture of wine yeasts and French oak barrels to produce clean, crisp wines that are magnificent companions with food. Between these two popular styles of Chardonnay are an infinite number of styles that are created with no oak influence (using stainless steel tanks), the use of more residual sugar for a softer palate feel and the blending of more inferior (and cheaper) grapes. Choosing between a $6 and a $60 Chardonnay introduces a world of mediocre bulk wine and super, great wines of traditional elegance. Let your palate and your pocketbook be your guide. It can be fun to explore your personal preferences. There is no better teacher than experience.

Q: I have had some Chablis wine from France and some from California. Why is there a big difference in price and quality between the two?

A: Chablis is probably the world's best known white wine and the authentic version comes from a small area about a hundred miles southeast of Paris. The region is named Chablis, and by international agreement only wine from that region, made with Chardonnay grapes under strict legal guidelines of the French government, is allowed to use the name. The United States, however, regards the name Chablis as generic identification for a type of wine. Usually, poor imitations of the real thing are made with lesser quality grapes and are marketed as inexpensive bulk wines.

Q: What is meant by the term *Fume Blanc*?

A: *Fume Blanc* is another term for the grape variety Sauvignon Blanc. The Robert Mondavi Winery is credited for commercially adopting the wording when it decided to come up with another name for the slow-selling Sauvignon Blanc wine. It caught on, and the wine has been a tremendous marketing success. Many other wineries also use the term, but all the attention to *Fume Blanc* led to the rediscovery of Sauvignon Blanc, which now is as popular as the *Fume Blanc* wines. They are, however, the same style of wine made from the same grape variety.

Q: A friend served me an imported wine that he said was called "Bull's Blood." It tasted pretty good, but what a weird name! Can you tell me anything about the wine?

A: What you experienced was *Bikaver*, a deep red, full-bodied red wine from the Hungarian village of Eger. The historic name of the wine is loosely translated as "bull's blood," but I assure you the popular-selling wine is made from local grapes.

Q: Is Cognac a liquor or a wine?

A: Legally, Cognac is classified as a liquor because it is a distilled spirit over twenty proof. Cognac is a brandy, however, from a designated district (Charente) in western France. Cognac, like brandy, is distilled from wine made from grapes.

Q: Are liqueurs and cordials wine-based or are they derived from distilled products?

A: Originally liqueurs, also known as cordials, are believed to have been wine-based with various herbs, roots, spices and peels added to flavor the drink. Today, most liqueurs start with distilled products from grapes, potatoes, grains or fruits, depending on the country where they are made. The blending of herbs, spices and other items are closely guarded secrets, even within the companies that make them. France and Italy are the leading manufacturers of liqueurs and have mastered the blending and marketing of the product over the centuries.

Q: Is vermouth a wine or just an ingredient for cocktails?

A: Vermouth is a white wine, usually fortified with some form of brandy and flavored with any number of herbs and spices. The two most popular versions are the French dry vermouths and the Italian sweet vermouths. California also produces its version of both types with considerable success. Vermouth is used primarily as an *apéritif* before dinner or as an ingredient for cocktails. Many chefs use vermouth as a flavor enhancement for signature sauces, as well.

Q: What is meant by the Solera in Solera Cream Sherry?

A: A Solera consist of rows of small, 50-gallon oak barrels stacked in tiers four high out in the open air. The sun slightly caramelizes the natural sugar in the wine just as it does for the fine sherries of Spain. In addition, there is a gentle, infinitely slow evaporation of moisture through the wood pores of the barrels, which tends to concentrate the flavors and richness of the wines within. A quarter to a third of the wine in the bottom barrels is removed for bottling and replaced by drawing down wine from the next tier up. This is repeated at each level until young wine is used to refill the top barrels. The traditional Solera is in essence an ancient form of fractional blending. Since the barrels are never emptied, some of the Solera's old, original wine always remains to add to its character.

Q: What are Alsatian wines?

A: Alsatian wines come from the French province of Alsace. Although French, this area, which borders the Rhine river, is definitely influenced by German culture. The vineyards of Alsace are some of the most picturesque in the world. The small towns are very quaint and storybook-like. The wines produced are almost exclusively white using the popular German grape varieties of Riesling and Gewürztraminer, as well as Pinot Blanc and Pinot Gris. Alsatian wines are very crisp, light and refreshing and are generally not quite as sweet as German wines.

Q: When we were in France we visited Alsace near the German border. The wines were very Germanic, but one white wine tasted like it might have had a little spice in it. What was it?

A: Though the German Riesling grape is widely grown in Alsace, I am sure you are referring to the area's noted Gewürztraminer (pronounced Geh-VIRTS trah-meen-eer) grape that does leave a slightly spicy taste in the flavor of the wine. The Gewürztraminer grape is also grown in the cooler areas of the Pacific Coast and in the Great Lakes Region of the United States quite successfully.

Q: I have a bottle of German wine with the term *spatlese* on it. What does it mean and what is the correct pronunciation?

A: *Spatlese* (SPATE-lay-zuh) literally means late picking. German wines made from late-harvested grapes carry this government-approved designation of *Qualitätswein mit Prädikat* (quality wine with special distinction). The next step up in quality is called *auslese* (ows-LAY-zuh) and are selected, late-picked grape bunches that make a sweet and spicy wine. Next comes *beerenauslese* (BEER-en-OWS-lay-zuh), which is wine made from individually selected, overripe berries. The highest, sweetest, rarest and most expensive of the German fine wine categories is *trockenbeerenauslese* (TRAWK-ken-BEER-en-OWS-lay-zuh), which literally means a wine made from a selection (*auslese*) of individually picked grapes (*beeren*) that have been left on the vine until so ripe as to be practically dry (*trocken*) or raisined. In the United States you will find similar wines with a "late harvest" or "selected bunch" designation on the label.

United States law forbids the use of foreign descriptive terminology on wine labels, unless the wine is of a universal or generic nature. The driest of the Prädikat wines is *Kabinett*, which is usually a light wine made of fully ripened grapes.

Q: What is Ice Wine?

A: Ice Wine is a Great Lakes style of sweet wine named after harvest conditions. The grapes are left ripening on the vine well into the winter season when they may be subject to a hard freeze. Since it is the water content of the grapes that freezes, the juice is a mixture of concentrated sugar, acidity and other flavor components. The grapes are gathered during the evening and early morning while they are still frozen and pressed immediately to separate the juice concentrate from the ice. After fermentation, the resulting wine is quite sweet with the capacity for a very long life. Originated in Germany, *Eiswein* is almost an accident of nature and not available in every harvest. Niagara-on-the Lake, Ontario, and New York's Finger Lakes produce some of the best Ice Wine in the world on a consistent basis.

Q: Are all the wines of Germany on the sweet side?

A: Definitely not. *Trocken*, or dry wines, have become increasingly more popular in both Europe and the United States to the point that the German wine industry has introduced two new designations to make it easier for consumers to identify the dry-style of German wines beyond *Kabinett*. Starting with the 2000 vintage, the "Classic" classification is applicable to the typical dry-style wines from a designated regional area. The new "Selection" designation applies to wines originating from an individual/single site where reduced yield and hand-selection harvest is practiced.

Q: I enjoy German white wine, such as Liebfraumilch and Piesporter. Are there any wines made in the United States that compare in taste?

A: The semi-dry, lower alcohol, German style of winemaking is quite common in wineries of the Great Lakes Region. They are also one of the most popular styles of wine in the tasting rooms. Because Germany and the Great Lakes Region have similar cool climate conditions, the wine grapes have a tendency to evolve to maturity before a high sugar level is reached. Since the sugar directly affects the alcohol content, these wines usually do not exceed 10%, as compared to other wines that normally reach 12 to 14%. The lake effect also creates, under certain conditions, a mold occurrence in the vineyards called *Botrytis Cinerea,* commonly referred to as "noble rot." This is a highly beneficial mold to certain types of grapes, bringing about a concentration of sugar and flavor in a high quality style of wine. Of course, there is no mold taste, only an elegantly sweet wine in the tradition of the great wines of Germany. Look for the grape varietal wines of Vidal, Vignoles or the classic Riesling with the label designation of Late Harvest, *Demi-Sec* or Reserve. There are also special "winery-blended" wines with some creative names that will remind you of some of the popular wines of Germany.

Q: I have some white table wines and Champagnes that I would like to put away for a while. How long will they keep?

A: Generally speaking, most white table wines and sparkling wines are at their peak by their third birthday. Of course, there are exceptions (e.g. Sauternes and German late-harvest wines). Again in general terms, the higher the alcohol content, the longer a wine will keep. Since most white and sparkling wines are lower in alcohol then red wines, they do not make good candidates for long-term collecting. Vintage Chardonnay and premium Champagnes do age quite well, although fifteen years would be stretching the limit. At this point, the wines lose their fruitiness and have a slight tinge of oxidation. Three to five years would be my suggestion for normal storage, with seven years being the limit for premium vintages and varieties.

Q: I am a big fan of Champagne. What makes this great celebration wine so special, and do they add sugar to get the different degrees of sweetness?

A: There is a mystique about Champagne that makes people want to save it for special occasions. Ironically, most Champagnes and sparkling wines are meant to be consumed and enjoyed early in their lives. Only a few exceptional vintage Champagnes will maintain their appeal over a few years. Champagne is the coldest, most northern of France's great wine growing regions and produces grapes of high acid and low alcohol potential. The character of the Champagne depends on the *dosage*. The *dosage* is a liqueur made of aged wine and various amounts of sugar that is added to the Champagne to form brut, extra dry, dry (*sec*) and sweet (*demi-sec*). Their terms are a little misleading. *Demi-sec* is the sweeter Champagne followed by dry, extra-dry and brut as the driest. Brut sparkling wines contain up to 1.5% residual sugar (the natural fruit sugar left in the finished wine after fermentation). Extra-Dry will have 1.5% to 3% residual sugar, while a *Demi-Sec* designation will be over 3%. Sparkling wines labeled Brut Sauvage, Extra Brut or Naturale will usually have under .5% residual sugar and give the sensation of being bone dry.

Q: I have a bottle of what I thought was French Champagne, but the label says *vins mousseux*. Is there a difference?

A: By French law, only sparkling wine made in the designated region of Champagne may use that term. Sparkling wines produced outside of the Champagne region are classified *vins mousseux* or "foamy wine." For your information, the entire European wine community also respects the French's claim to their wine term "Champagne." As a result, German sparkling wines are known as *sekt;* Spanish sparkling wines are identified as *cava;* and the popular Italian sparkling wines are marketed as *spumante*. United States regulations allow winemakers to use the word Champagne as generic terminology, provided the geographic location in which it is made precedes the name, such as "New York Champagne." Other sparkling wine terms seen on premium labels in the United States are *Blanc de Blanc, Blanc de Noir,* or simply Sparkling Wine.

Q: What is the meaning of a wine labeled *Blanc de Blancs?*

A: *Blanc de Blancs* is French for white wine made from white grapes. It is used quite frequently as a reference for American-made sparkling wines. You may also come across the term *Blanc de Noir,* which means white wine made from black grapes by fermenting the must without the skins present. All grape juice is clear. The color of wine comes from the pigment of the grape skins.

Q: I have noticed that some bottles of Champagne have the words *methode champenoise* on them and others say *charmat* process. What is the difference?

A: There are three ways to make Champagne. The first is *methode champenoise*, or the method of the Champagne region, which is also the most expensive. This process involves a second fermentation of wine in the bottle after the addition of a small amount of sugar and yeast. Champagne bubbles are the gases from fermentation that are unable to escape. Since this process is labor intensive and time consuming, the price goes up. The second process is called *charmat*, or bulk. The same thing happens to the wine, except it takes place in large, sealed tanks and is drawn off into bottles under pressure. This requires less manpower and less time to produce a sparkling wine. The third, and much less expensive process for making sparkling wine, is simply to inject CO_2 carbonation into a still wine—with less spectacular quality results.

Q: What is *cremant*? How is it different from Cramant?

A: *Cremant*, a French term, literally translated means creaming. It is applied to wines that are lightly sparkling. Some connoisseurs prefer a superior *cremant* to Champagne because of the subtle sparkle in the wine. Do not confuse *cremant* for Cramant, an important wine-producing village in the Champagne region of France.

Q: Any special advice for serving Champagne?

A: First and foremost, be careful opening the bottle. Slowly remove the cork with the aid of a towel to keep it from flying and to absorb any spillage. Sparkling wines should be served well-chilled and in flute or tulip-style glasses for full enjoyment. Avoid the flat, saucer-shaped glasses. These so-called "traditional Champagne glasses" allow the bubbles to dissipate too quickly and the fun is gone much too soon. In either case, nothing adds to a festive occasion like the bubbles of a sparkling wine.

Q: I have a bottle of 1975 Champagne Brut, G.H. Mumm and Company, Reims, France. How do I tell if the wine is good or not?

A: You have an excellent vintage of Champagne from one of the top producers in France. The vintage and producer are very important factors in the quality of any older wine. Providing the wine has been cared for and stored properly, it should still be drinkable, although the signs of age will be evident in the color and taste. There is only one sure way to find out, and today is as good a day as any to try it.

Q: I am a bit concerned with the storage of my Champagne. I have read that Champagne is not conducive to long term storage once it has been released from the winery. I like to keep a case or two of Bollinger around for about a year or so. Is there any danger of this Champagne going bad?

A: It is true that most sparkling wines are best imbibed within a couple of years after they have been released by the winery, but it all depends on the quality of the wine and the conditions under which it has been stored. Your storage of the premium Bollinger Champagne for only a year or so is no problem, provided the storage area is free of extreme heat variation, excessive vibration or bright lights. Wine does not go bad overnight, and you will be able to taste the change when it begins to lose its elegance.

Q. Please settle a discussion on Champagne grapes. My friend says a multitude of grapes are used, including the red grape Pinot Noir. I argue that Chardonnay is the grape of true Champagne. Who is right?

A: French Champagne is made from a blend of grapes and vintages that include both Chardonnay and Pinot Noir, as well as Pinot Blanc and a minor red grape called Pinot Meunier. At the time of the harvest crush the red grapes are pressed and separated from their skins so the juice will remain clear for the making of Champagne. *Blanc de Blanc* wines are sparkling wines that are made exclusively of white grapes and predominantly Chardonnay. The exact *cuvée* or blend of juices is a closely guarded formula by each of the great houses of Champagne.

Q: While touring a famous Champagne cellar in France, I was mesmerized watching the winery's riddler turning the bottles. How many do these pros turn in a day?

A: Although the tendency these days is to mechanically turn Champagne bottles, many of the old Champagne houses still employ professional riddlers for the traditional handling of *methode champenoise* wine bottles. Riddling is the turning of Champagne bottles a quarter turn every day to force sediment to the neck of the bottle where it is then frozen and removed from the bottle. The average number of bottles of Champagne a cellar worker is expected to riddle by hand each day is around 50,000. Whew!

Q: What is Cassis and Kir Royale?

A: Creme de Cassis is a very rich and full flavored liqueur made from black currants. Its origin is France, as is Kir Royale, which is the addition of Cassis to Champagne. Plain Kir is simply white wine mixed at about six parts with one part Cassis. Kir and Kir Royale are quite popular in Europe as a before dinner drink to stimulate the appetite. Raspberry and cherry wines also lend themselves quite appropriately to this elegant wine cocktail.

Q: What are blush wines?

A: In recent years the making of blush wines has become extremely popular. Most of these wines are made from red grapes whose skins are separated from the juice very early in the winemaking process. The result is a light-bodied wine with a light red hue that falls in between rosé and white categories. The most popular example is White Zinfandel, which is made from the red grape, Zinfandel.

Q: Why do wines come in differently shaped bottles?

A: The evolution of the glass bottle as a part of the traditions and culture of each wine-producing region is long and interesting, but a quick explanation of what you may expect from the shape and color of wine bottles on your merchant's shelves can be helpful. The high-shouldered, straight-sided Bordeaux bottle is the most common shape of all. It is used in almost all wine-producing countries. Green glass is used for red wine and clear glass for whites. This bottle shape represents the classic Bordeaux soft styles of dry reds and dry or sweet whites.

A slope-shouldered bottle hints of a full-bodied red wine characterized by the wines of Burgundy and the robust wines of Italy's famed Piedmont region. The full-flavored whites of Chablis and Chardonnay are also found in this bottle shape.

The tall slender bottle, restyled from the Burgundy shape, is brown for most German Rhine style wines, but green for the more delicate and fragrant Moselle and Alsatian-style wines. Sherries and Ports appear in the narrow-waisted bottles that are the traditional shape for dessert wines and have generally been accepted worldwide for this style of wine. The color of bottles is determined primarily by regional tradition, but any colored bottle is used to protect the wine from an overexposure of light.

Q: Are restaurant house wines a good value?

A: Sometimes yes, and sometimes no. I do not mean to sound evasive, but you do need more information about what is being poured as the house wine. Astute restaurant managers use house or featured wines as a promotional vehicle to introduce you to their wine list and menu. These wines are usually very good values and should be sought out whenever possible. However, many restaurants are interested only in getting the maximum profit out of a glass or carafe of wine by serving the lowest priced wine they can buy without concern for quality and value. I am all for making an honest profit, but charging several more times the wholesale cost is excessive in my opinion. Ask what type and brand of wine is being served as the house wine and if no one knows, be wary!

Q: I understand that early colonists found native Scuppernong grapes when they arrived and made their first homemade wine from them. Is there still Scuppernong wine available in the United States?

A: Scuppernong grapes are indeed from a native American vine. The vines have been known to exist for centuries in the Carolinas, Florida and the Gulf States. To make wine from the Scuppernong requires the addition of a large amount of sugar, with results that are not considered to be the ultimate in quality. With a little research, you will find Scuppernong wine still being made in a few southeastern states.

Q: Is the term Reserve on a wine label something special or is it just a marketing ploy?

A: In Italy and Spain the term *Reserva* or *Riserva* has a very specific and legal meaning. In these countries the term is applied to wines that have been aged longer than the rest of the wines from that vintage. Wine producers traditionally apply the term only to the top quality wines that have been given special treatment and care. In the United States, label designations like "winemaker's reserve" and "vintage select" also have become a sign of special quality wines. Unlike Europe, however, there are no specific legal guidelines and a few United States producers will use the terminology as a marketing tool. A good test of reliability is to remember the special care and handling involved in the making of these wines. They are expensive to produce, so you will not likely find a true reserve for $4.99.

Q: About twenty years ago my son brought back from Spain a bottle of Dry Sack sherry wine. The bottle label does not have a date on it. Is it still drinkable?

A: Dry Sack is a top selling wine from the famous and first-class sherry *bodega* (Spanish for winery or wine cellar). The label does not carry a vintage date because sherry is a blend of wines and vintages in order to maintain a consistent product. Your Dry Sack is a medium Amontillado (as in Edgar Allen Poe's "The Cask of Amontillado") and is a superior type of sherry, generally fairly dry and pale. Since Spanish sherry is a wine that is fortified with grape brandy to bring the alcohol content up to 20% and thus acts as a preservative, I am confident the wine is quite drinkable. Be advised, however, that once you open the bottle it will deteriorate within a relatively short time. And remember; sherry does not improve with age after it has been bottled.

Q: Will you tell me something about the Semillon grape variety?

A: Semillon (say-me-ohn) is a very important grape in France's Bordeaux region. As a dry table wine it is often blended with Sauvignon Blanc to produce Graves and Bordeaux Blanc wines. In Sauternes it is the principal grape for their famous sweet dessert wines. The Aussies blend the soft Semillon with Chardonnay for their popular Sem-Chard style of Australian table wine that is much mellower than a full-bodied Chardonnay. On the Pacific coast of the United States the cooler climate of Washington creates a hospitable home for the rich (honey and clover) and fruity (figs and apricots) wine grape. Semillon is an excellent companion for herbed chicken, shellfish and seafood.

Q: I have tasted some wines from Hungary and Bulgaria. Although they were not of the quality of Lafite, they were quite drinkable and inexpensive. How can they produce and ship the wine so cheaply?

A: Baltic countries such as Hungary and Bulgaria are able to compete in the world marketplace with the help of very large government subsidies, plus low labor and land costs. And you are right, the winemaking expertise of these countries does not produce a quality product even close to the great Bordeaux.

Q: I have a bottle of Beaujolais Nouveau wine from the 2001 harvest. I know it should be drunk young, but when will it be "over-the-hill?"

A: The French Beaujolais Nouveau is released the third week in November and is intended to be enjoyed through the Christmas holidays. Chances are the wine is still drinkable, but has more than likely lost the fresh, fruitful luster that makes this wine so appealing. It is a fun wine to be enjoyed almost immediately. United States versions of this popular French wine style live longer and become more complex table wines, but are still not considered wines to put away in storage.

Q: Please give us some information about the French/American hybrid wine grapes called Vignoles and Vidal Blanc. They seem to be quite popular in the vineyards of Eastern states.

A: In the late 1880s, the grafting of French vines on American root stock created a productive and sturdy vine that was able to withstand the attack of a tiny pest called *phylloxera*. This technique was responsible for saving the European wine industry from devastation at the time. Today, cross-breeding continues to produce quality grapevines that prosper in cooler climates. One such variety is Vignoles. From the northern regions its aroma and flavor are citrusy. From the southern vineyards Vignoles wines have pineapple characteristics. The grape is very versatile, yielding impressive wine in full, dry, semi-dry or sweet styles. Vignoles has been aged successfully in oak, and is considered one of the best white hybrid varieties in Eastern America. Vidal Blanc is another French hybrid variety that offers a lovely fruit character in the popular reserve or *demi-sec* style. Vidal Blanc has a cool, green, herbaceous aspect to it that proves most refreshing. Vidal, along with Riesling, are responsible for some of the fantastic Ice Wines being produced in Ontario, Canada, and in New York's Finger Lakes Region.

Q: What makes United States hybrid grape varieties different from European grapes?

A: The French-American grape varieties you refer to are the result of carefully selected crosses between European *vinifera* and native American grape vines. Most were developed in agricultural research centers in France, Italy and New York State. The goal has been to increase adaptability to the environment of Eastern United States growing regions by increasing resistance to extreme cold, insects, diseases, mildews, etc., while achieving optimum production of quality grapes for winemaking. So far, I would say they have done a pretty good job not only with wine grapes, but with many other fruit, grain and vegetable hybrid crop varieties as well. Many of these so-called hybrid grapes trace over 50% of their parentage to European varieties. For example, the versatile Vignoles grape claims one of its direct parents as Pinot Noir, a highly regarded variety from Champagne and Burgundy. The popular Great Lakes Vidal Blanc's heritage is directly connected to the widely used Italian grape known as Trebbiano. The hybrid varieties of Seyval, Foch and Chancellor also have a strong

European heritage in their development. Maybe hybrid grape varieties are not so different from European vines, after all. Besides, it is the end result that counts.

Q: The French/American hybrid wine grapes in the Eastern United States regions are a success. Did the French or the Americans develop the vines?

A: After the plant louse *phylloxera* epidemic in Europe a century ago, a number of France's leading biologists began breeding hybrid vines by marrying the European classics to *phylloxera*-resistant American species. Once they mastered the technique of grafting French originals onto American roots, and thereby solving the dreaded insect problem, they abandoned any further development of hybrids. The new hybrids were found to be hardy, disease resistant and productive, and the wines made from them were of excellent quality. Because of these attributes, the vines were much more suitable to the growing conditions of eastern North America than were most of the European varieties. Further research and development of the hybrid varieties was conducted at the Geneva Agricultural Station in New York State. Many of the hybrid varieties are also very popular in the new vineyards of England and New Zealand.

Q: Which of the following French hybrid grape varieties are used for white wine: Seyval, Chancellor, Vidal, Vignoles, De Chaunac and Foch?

A: Seyval (say-voll), Vidal (vee-doll), and Vignoles (vin-yole) are the three primary French hybrid grapes used to make white wines from very dry to semisweet. Chancellor and Foch (foe-shh) are premium red grapes. De Chaunac (day-shawn-uc) is a red grape that makes an excellent rosé wine as well as a red table wine.

Q: Virtually every region in Italy produces wine, but where does the best Italian wine come from?

A: Many feel the wines of the Piedmonte region in northwestern Italy produce not only Italy's finest, but *Barolo, Barbaresco* and *Grignolino* rank among the best in the world. Fans of *Chianti Classico Riserva* and *Brunello di Montalcino* from the Tuscany region will also put up a strong argument for their wines.

Q: Is there such a thing as an American Chianti?

A: Technically, Chianti is the popular dry red wine from the Tuscany region near Florence, Italy. The primary grape used in making Chianti is Sangiovese. Inexpensive jug imitations of Chianti have been produced for years in wine areas that have large Italian settlements such as California and Argentina. Much of the early Chianti that was imported to the United States in straw *fiasco* baskets was of inferior quality. Since the 1980s, however, the quality of Chianti Classico and Riserva wines rival many of the world's finest. In the last decade, the Sangiovese grape has become popular with California growers and winemakers with some excellent results. If you are looking for an American Chianti, try some of the more recent Sangiovese wines from California.

Q: What are Veronese wines?

A: I assume you are referring to the wines of the Veneto region around Lake Garda and Verona, Italy. The popular wines of Soave, Valpolicella and Bardolino have made Verona one of the most important wine capitals in Italy. The characteristically fruity wines are soft, pleasant table wines best consumed very young. The better Amarones of the Valpolicella zone are rich, complex and can improve with age for well over ten years.

Q: What does *classico* mean on the labels of Italian wines?

A: *Classico* is the term used for a restricted area within an officially designated appellation or *denominazione di origine controllata* (DOC). The *classico* region is traditionally located in the heart of the particular growing area and usually offers the best wines produced in that DOC. Chianti Classico is probably the most famous of the Italian *classico* regions.

Q: What is the difference between *Spumante* and Asti Spumante?

A: *Spumante* is the Italian word for sparkling. Asti is a prominent wine producing town south of Turin in the Piedmont region of Italy and is particularly famous for its somewhat sweet sparkling wine. When the label says Asti Spumante it identifies the sparkling wine as the sweeter version produced in this region. Plain *Spumante* could have come from anywhere and may even be dry or brut. It is generally considered that the best *Spumante* comes from the town of Asti.

Q: What is the correct pronunciation of the Riesling grape and wine. Also, how is Merlot pronounced?

A: Riesling is pronounced REECE_ LING with a long "e." The grape variety Merlot is pronounced with a silent "t" — MAIR_ LOW.

Q: What kind of wine is a Claret?

A: "Claret" is a very old British nickname for the dry red wines of Bordeaux. For centuries England was the primary market for Bordeaux wines and with time the term became commonplace within the trade and still exists in European markets. The term, however, is not commonly used in the United States.

Q: What gives port its unusual flavor? Why is it so dramatically different from any other wines?

A: *Porto* originated in Portugal and was made famous as one of the world's finest *aperitif* and dessert wines by the English. The production of port starts much the same as any other wine with the juice of crushed grapes placed in tanks and the addition of a yeast culture to stimulate fermentation. When the desired degree of alcohol has been attained, brandy is added. This brings the alcohol content up to the desired 20% level and stops the process, allowing the "fortified" wine to retain a sweet taste due to the unconverted residual grape sugars still in the wine. Aging takes place in both wood and bottles depending on the winemakers decision as to the wine's style. Some excellent ports (as opposed to the Portuguese *Porto*) are made across the United States.

Q: What is the difference between White Zinfandel and plain Zinfandel wines?

A: First of all, White Zinfandel is not a white wine. It falls in the category of blush wines, which is a phenomena that was spearheaded by Sutter Home Winery in the 1980s. The Zinfandel grape is a red grape that traditionally produces a wine of intense flavor without being overpowering. Secondly, the juice of virtually all grapes is clear. The juice extracts its color from the skin pigments of crushed grapes (the must) during fermentation. When the juice is separated from the must early in the fermentation process the result is a salmon or pinkish color left on the wine, which is then marketed as White Zinfandel as opposed to the traditional red Zinfandel.

Q: What is the difference between *Pinot Gris* and *Pinot Grigio*?

A: A simple answer is language. *Pinot Gris* (French) and *Pinot Grigio* (Italian) are the same grape. American producers will use both terms on their labels, depending on their marketing approach. The excellent, full-bodied, dry white wine of Oregon is almost exclusively labeled *Pinot Gris*. Some Eastern United States winemakers have picked up on the name *Pinot Grigio* hoping to take advantage of the popularity of Italy's lighter winemaking style of the grape.

Q: What is mulled wine?

A: Mulled or spiced wines have been a favorite of outdoor winter enthusiasts for many years. They usually consist of red wine flavored with a variety of herbs and spices, such as cinnamon and cloves, and served hot in a coffee mug to ward off the bone-chilling cold of winter. You can purchase prepackaged spices and add them to your inexpensive jug wine, or bottles of mulled wine from the winery are available at retail shops. Spiced wine can be a real party treat served with a cinnamon stick in front of the fireplace on a blustery winter evening.

Q: What is "noble rot" in reference to wine?

A: "Noble rot" is the English nickname for the Latin name *Botrytis Cinerea*, which is a form of mold that attacks the skins of ripe grapes in vineyards under certain conditions of warm and misty autumn weather. *Botrytis*-affected grapes cause a concentration of sugar while the fruit's water evaporates. The results are some of the most luscious dessert wines in the world. This natural phenomenon occurs in good vintages in Sauternes, the Rhine, the Mosel, Tokaji in Hungary and in certain areas of the Great Lakes Region. Since hand-harvesting the withered grape bunches yields a restricted amount of juice, the price is usually more expensive than regular wines.

Winemaking

Wine is one of the most civilized things in the
world and one of the natural things that has
been brought to the greatest perfection.
It offers a greater range for enjoyment
and appreciation than possibly any other
purely sensory thing that
can be purchased.

ERNEST HEMINGWAY

•

I love the sound of a popping cork.
I know then, that the waiting is over
and it's time to enjoy.

JOE BORRELLO

Q: How many acres of grape vines are planted in the world?

A: At last count, there are over 22 million acres planted and the number is still growing. Rest assured, there is plenty of wine for everyone.

Q: What determines when the wine process is complete at the winery and the finished product is ready to be released to the public?

A: Making wine is not just an art. It is also a science requiring precise procedures and controls, combined with personal judgment and assessment based on hundreds of sensory experiences and evaluations. Whether or not a wine is ready for bottling or release to the public is a matter of judgment. Scientific procedures and equipment can assist the vintner in making the wine and aging it properly, but the day comes when the winemaker must rely on the basic senses of sight, taste and smell. Drawing on his or her knowledge and years of experience, the vintner pronounces the wine ready to leave the winery and be welcomed, opened and enjoyed on the tables of wine drinkers everywhere.

Q: What is the difference between grapes used for wine and those for sale in the produce department of the grocery store?

A: The primary difference between the two is sugar level. Table grapes are harvested at about 15% sugar with higher acid levels that give a refreshing taste when eaten. The grape varieties designated to produce wine are left to ripen to over 20% sugar so that the fermentation process will produce juice with 10-14% alcohol.

Q: I remember as a child helping my grandfather pick and crush grapes to make wine. Today everything looks to be highly mechanized. Is wine made in the old traditional way by hand any more?

A: Almost all of the small wineries in the world still rely on manual labor to harvest their crops. Only the very large operations find it economical to invest in mechanical pickers and other labor-saving machines. Although the practice of grape stomping is virtually extinct, it is still practiced for show at festivals and for tourists at wineries. Even with the modernization of equipment, not much changed in the process of making wine for centuries, until the last few decades. Today, even the old-timers are paying attention to scientific research on the growing of vines, the intricacies of natural chemistry involved with winemaking and various techniques available to increase the quality of production. A scientific approach to agriculture is more the rule in most wine-growing regions around the world, reducing guesswork and chance. Until someone learns how to control Mother Nature, however, grape-growing and winemaking will still be product of land, weather and hard hands-on work.

Q: How many pounds of grapes can a vineyard worker pick on a good day during harvest?

A: According to the *St. Helena Star* in California, a worker will pick nearly two tons of grapes in a day's work.

Q: What makes some areas more conducive to wine-grape growing than others?

A: Everything revolves around the right geography, air currents, soil drainage, and light, all of which are vital to growing quality wine grapes. Large bodies of water, like the ocean, have an important influence on the temperature in certain geographic areas called micro-climates. Cool winds from the water in early spring help prevent buds from opening until the danger of frost has passed. The opposite occurs in the late fall when prevailing winds provide warmth for the vineyards and extend the growing season. In cooler climate areas like the Great Lakes Region in the United States, deep winter snows also provide vine protection from subzero temperatures,

Q: Is there really that much difference between a bottle of $5 wine and one that costs $50?

A: Like any consumer product, the price of wine is often determined by supply and demand. Production techniques also play an important part in the cost of wines. For instance, wines that offer subtlety and charm generally cannot be produced as economically as simple table wines, since they require selective soils and severely restrained vineyard yields to concentrate flavor and quality. These wines possess complexities derived from painstaking winemaking that usually adds to the cost of production. For those who really enjoy wine, the price is worth the added dimension these limited production wines offer. Many United States wines are produced using these methods, but they may not be as well known or as expensive as their European cousins. The worldwide value of the United States dollar also plays a major role in the price of imports — and that has nothing to do with the quality of the wine. Makes you think about comparing taste and value, doesn't it?

Q: I have read that extended periods of no rain do not hurt established vineyards because of their deep-rooted system. How come I saw sprinkler systems operating in some vineyards in California this spring, if not for irrigation?

A: The sprinkler system was not for irrigation, but rather for frost protection. In the spring there is always the threat of frost until mid-May. Basically, the sprinkler system utilizes a network of underground water pipes spaced throughout the vineyard to which are attached vertical pipes with a special sprinkler head at the top of each. When temperatures fall near the freezing point these sprinklers are turned on, sending a fine mist over the vineyard, which then freezes at 32º F. When water freezes it gives off heat, thus the ice-coated leaves and tender shoots of the vine remain at 32ºF even though the air temperature may continue to fall another 5 degrees or so. As long as the sprinklers remain on, the vines are protected. The same effect is experienced in Eastern United States wine regions with winter snows. Both the freezing ice and the snow act as insulators for the fragile vines against very low air temperatures.

Q: Please explain what people mean when they say, "This wine has a lot of tannin in it."

A: The astringent or bitter qualities in wines come from tannins, a natural component found in grape skins. White wines acquire tannins during skin contact and pressing, red wines during fermentation. In some wines, tannin is also added by aging in oak barrels. Tannin acts as a preservative that helps prolong the life of some wines, but it makes them unappealing to drink until some of the tannin has settled out with age. Young, tannic red wines demonstrate astringency, drying the mouth and leaving a rough feeling on the tongue and teeth. A white wine with too much tannin will have a bitter finish. Visually, tannin forms part of the natural sediment found in the bottom of the bottle.

Q: Why do the Greeks put resin in their wine? It tastes awful.

A: Before bottles were invented, wine was stored and transported in animal skins, usually pig or goat. The Greeks would line the inside of the skins with pitch (resin) to prevent leakage and help preserve the wine. Obviously, the strong essence of resin would flavor the wine. The Greeks got used to it and continued to add it to their wine even when the skins were replaced by bottles. Like many alcoholic concoctions, *Retsina* is an acquired taste.

Q: What is the difference between aroma and bouquet when it comes to wine appreciation?

A: Wine's aroma is derived from the specific grape variety. The ability to distinguish one wine type from another is influenced by the distinctiveness of the grape's natural odor. Bouquet originates from the fermentation process, aging and general production of the wine. Bouquet may be described as woody, yeasty, earthy, vegetative, moldy, oxidized and any number of other terms favorable or not. The ability to recognize these various odor components is the result of experience, concentration while tasting and memory.

Q: What is the white waxy substance found on the outside of just picked grapes?

A: The white waxy substance on grapes are yeast cells which consume the natural sugars in the grape's juice. The yeasts convert the sugar, through fermentation, to roughly equal parts of carbon dioxide and alcohol. This is one of Mother Nature's first steps in the process of making wine. If you were to mash those grapes in a bucket and leave them alone for a couple of days, they would be well on their way to making a batch of wine all by themselves.

Q: How big an effect does weather have on wine production from one year to the next?

A: You can look at that question from two sides. If you are the grower, Mother Nature is your business partner and your competitor. Spring frosts, pests, plant disease and fall rains could all spell disaster for the crop in any one year. The timing and amount of rain and sunshine also contribute greatly to plant development, and ultimately to the quality of the wine from that particular crop. As you can imagine, yields and quality do vary from harvest to harvest. From the customer's point of view, we can always substitute wine from an area that had a bad year with one that had better results. Since the world's wine growing regions are so vast and separate from each other, there is usually good wine produced somewhere.

Q: How does barrel aging come into play with the development of premium wines?

A: Wines meant for continued aging (such as Cabernet Sauvignon, Pinot Noir and Chardonnay) are immature, rough and reflect the simple fruit of the grape when taken from the fermenting tanks. The transformation of a young wine to a mature, complex one starts in the barrel and is completed through bottle aging. During oak aging, the sharp, fruity, fermented wine softens into more appealing and refined flavors. The barrel allows a slow penetration of air into the wine, permitting aging to occur. At the same time, it imparts a small amount of oak character that marries with the wine and adds complexity. The traditional 60-gallon oak barrel is the optimum size for balancing wine aging through air penetration and the oak character acquired by the wine. A larger barrel or tank lacks sufficient wine/wood contact, while a smaller barrel may contribute too much oak before the wine has had adequate time to mature.

Q: What is the difference between wines that say "barrel-fermented" on the label versus labels that say "barrel-aged?"

A: Although most wine is fermented in large stainless steel tanks, some special premium wines are fermented in oak barrels (50-60 gallon size) where the wood interaction imparts some special flavor elements that add to the wine's complexity. This is an expensive and labor-intensive method and is therefore usually reserved for only high quality juice. Similar, though less intensive results may be obtained by fermenting the juice in stainless steel tanks and then transferring the wine to oak barrels, where the wine is left to age for a period of time. To label a bottle "barrel-fermented," 100% of the wine in the bottle must have gone through the barrel-fermenting process. The label term of "barrel (or oak) aged" has no legal definition and so the results of aging could vary widely. As usual in the making of wine, the winemaker determines the process and the final style.

Q: Why is wine aged in wood?

A: Wine extracts certain elements from the wood. Flavor components, aromatic substances and wood tannins all contribute to the body, character and complexity of the wine, particularly premium red wines. Oak wood barrels have been the choice of winemakers for centuries to add the finishing touches to fine red or white wines and to give them the extra qualities that allow them to develop and improve with age. Although wood is porous, well-constructed barrels let in just the right amount of oxygen, aiding the formation of esters, which change the flavor of the wine beneficially, softening and mellowing it.

Q: While visiting wineries, I noticed some of the storage tanks were made of wood and some of steel. What is the difference?

A: Stainless steel provides an airtight container while wood, more specifically oak, offers a porous surface. The stainless steel is used when the winemaker wishes to produce a wine (usually white) that maintains the fruitiness of the grape, whereas oak-aged wines (primarily red) develop a complex structure due to the minute passage of air through the wood pores. Depending on the age and size of the container, stored wine will also pick up certain flavor and aging nuances from the wood. Stainless steel tanks permit better temperature control of the tanks than do the wooden varieties. Wood, however, is the favored medium of winemakers for long-term aging of wine where subtle flavors and complexity are the desired effects.

Q: What do wineries mean when they say they rack the wine?

A: Racking is the movement of wine from one container to another. This is a natural and traditional method of wine clarification by which precipitated solids are left behind with each movement of the wine. These solids are the natural residual deposits of the winemaking process and continue sometimes in the bottle. This is why it is often recommended to decant an older wine into a clean, clear decanter before serving it to your guests. These deposits are in no way harmful, but they do taste bitter.

Q: On a winery tour the guide said that workers enter the large wine tanks from a small hole on the bottom to clean it out. How can an adult get through an opening no bigger than eighteen or twenty inches?

A: When wine is moved from one tank to another it will leave small particles of grape solids, skins and yeast that have settled on the bottom and sides of the tank. It is necessary to sanitize the inside of these tanks and barrels before new wine can be placed in them. The use of pressure and suction hoses removes most of the residual, but the final step necessitates the placement of someone into the tank to inspect it. There is a trick to it. It is done by first placing the arms over the head. You then insert one shoulder, followed by the other, at which point you push yourself through. Using the proper technique, even quite a large person can enter a tank without great difficulty.

Q: During a winery tour the guide mentioned a wine thief. What is a wine thief?

A: It isn't a masked bandit, if that's what you mean. But it is a device to "steal" the wine from the barrel for testing. A wine thief is a simple hollow tube, usually made of glass or stainless steel, that is inserted through the bung hole of a barrel to withdraw a sample of the wine. This is a daily process for the winemaker in determining when the wine is ready to bottle or for extracting samples for one of the laboratory analyses that are constantly being conducted at the winery.

Q: I opened a bottle of white wine that had some crystals on the bottom of the cork and in the bottom of the bottle. What is it, and is it harmless?

A: The crystals are the result of tartaric acid, which is the principal acid in wine made from ripe grapes. They are not harmful and are natural deposits of the wine. This suspicious looking substance is also known as cream of tartar. It is a by-product of the wine used in the manufacture of baking powder. If you find an accumulation of cream of tartar crystals in a bottle of wine, you need only allow the material to settle to the bottom and carefully pour off the clear wine into a clean, fresh container. Now you can enjoy your wine with complete peace of mind. By the way, here's a little household hint for cleaning a greasy aluminum pan with cream of tartar: Add one tablespoon of cream of tartar to the pan filled with water and boil it for a few minutes. Rinse and wipe clean. Wine works wonders — even with its by-products.

Q: How many bottles of wine can be filled by a barrel of wine?

A: Though the size of barrels vary slightly (the classic French barrel is called a *barrique*), there are approximately 300 standard 750ml bottles of wine in a barrel.

Q: Why are grape vines pruned back so severely in the winter?

A: Grape vines are cut back or pruned so as to form and train the vine for a specific purpose. That purpose may be to produce higher quality, increase production, or promote a longer life cycle for the vine itself. Pruning in the vineyards is a science and literally hundreds of books have been written on the subject. For the most part, pruning controls over-production of the vine and encourages higher quality grapes. Every vine in the vineyard is hand-pruned down to one or two small branches from the main trunk. It is a cold, tedious job but one that most winemakers consider a necessity for quality control of the grape production.

Q: What is the average life span of a grape vine?

A: About 25 years, on average. Some, however, have been known to live 50 to 100 years or more. The prime fruit-producing years are after ten harvests and under thirty-five. After that the vines still produce quality fruit, but not as vigorously and plentiful.

Q: Do winemakers consider wine and food combinations when making their products? Some wines seem to overpower food instead of complementing it.

A: Although research and experimentation are highly advisable for climate and soil adaptations, some producers have indeed crossed the lines of tradition by making intense wines that overemphasize the use of wood, fruit and alcohol. I have seen, however, a gradual return to the customary methods of producing wines with elegance and balance. As with most consumer products, the customer speaks the loudest and they are purchasing table wines with finesse and smoothness that complement food instead of conflicting with it. After hundreds of years of research and experimentation, traditional winemaking has not changed much. Wine and food with family and friends still remain the classic ingredients of a gracious dinner.

Q: On a wine label, it said the grapes were picked at 21 *brix*. What is a *brix*?

A: *Brix* (pronounced bricks) is a measurement scale by which winemakers measure sugar content. Dividing the *brix* by two will give you a rough estimate of the potential alcohol obtained through fermentation. For instance, with grapes picked at 21 *brix*, the resulting wine would have about 10 to 11 percent alcohol if the winemaker allowed the juice to completely ferment. The *brix* is only one element in the winemaker's decision about when to pick and crush the grapes. Weather forecasts at the time of harvest are also crucial.

Q: What is meant by the pH factor in wine?

A: The pH of a wine is a measurement of the active acids. The lower the pH, the more acidic, sharp or clean a wine will taste. A wine with high pH will taste flat or lacking in acidity. A pH measurement of around 3.5

or lower is about normal for most wines. Fairly low pH in wines is important not only for taste, but also for wine stability since a low pH tends to naturally inhibit spoilage. The pH of a wine also affects its color. Red wines with low pH appear more red, while high pH wines have a blue/purple cast even when quite old. A high pH wine will not only lack crispness, it may also have "off" flavors, the most common being a metallic tin can taste. A high pH will also contribute to producing a vinegar smell in the wine.

Q: I have noticed that some local wine labels do not declare the alcohol content of its wine. Are small wineries exempt from this BATF requirement?

A: The Bureau of Alcohol, Tobacco and Firearms (BATF) requires all wine labels to state the alcohol content on the bottle (with a tolerance of 1 1/2 percent, either way) or to simply print the words "table wine" prominently on the label. The BATF considers that these words indicate the bottled wine contains 7 to 14% alcohol. Wineries that produce a non-vintage proprietary wine that is blended from year to year save money in printing costs when they do not have to reprint a new label each year with different information. It is just a matter of economics for small wineries — not an exemption.

Q: How do wineries control fruit flies when they make wine?

A: You are correct in assuming that wineries are inundated with fruit flies, especially during harvest time. It is specifically for this reason that wineries are continually washing down containers, equipment and winery floors. As you tour a winery, for instance, you will notice a network of drains throughout the winery that allow for constant sterilization with a steady stream of water and chlorine. You may also notice large fans that keep air circulating and cause navigational problems for the lightweight critters. Once the fruit begins fermenting in open tanks, the continuous flow of escaping gases drives away any living thing. In the unlikely event fruit flies have fought their way to the floating "must" of grape skins at the top of the tank, the wine is removed from the bottom and micro-filtered. The wine is always in sealed containers from that point on. After the harvest, fruit flies hang around for any wine that escapes from the tanks or transfer hoses. Hence, the year-round attention to sanitary procedures.

Q: What was the insect that nearly destroyed all the vineyards in Europe in the late nineteenth century? Is it true that native American grape vines were used to prevent the disaster?

A: The destructive creature you are asking about is named *phylloxera* (fill-lox-er-ra) and in the 1860s this plant louse destroyed over two million acres of vineyards in France alone. The *phylloxera* is native to the eastern part of the United States and was accidentally transplanted to Europe, more than likely on experimental vines. It rampaged the vineyards of Europe unchecked for nearly two decades. Since native American vines are resistant to *phylloxera*, out of desperation of losing the entire grape industry, growers grafted American rootstock to European vine cuttings as a last chance effort. It worked, and today literally every grape vine in Europe is an extension of American rootstock. You might say that if it were not for American rootstock there would be no French wines. On the other hand, if it were not for the American pest, there would not have been a problem in the first place.

Q: How accurate are vintage dates of wine bottles? Don't wineries blend different years to maintain consistency?

A: Wineries do sometimes blend wines of different years to maintain a consistency in style. However, as of 1983, the United States government decreed that all wines that do use a vintage date must contain at least 95% of the wine of that particular harvest year.

Q: What would be the rough cost of starting a winery?

A: According to some vineyard developers we spoke with, first you must purchase about twice as many acres of land as you wish to plant in order to get the plantable acreage you need. That will cost anywhere from $2,000 to $80,000 per acre, depending on the popularity and availability of the land in the desired area. Once the land has been cleared and planted, it will take five years of maintenance to develop a vineyard capable of producing a crop that will eventually bring back a return on your investment. If you set up a management contract with a local farmer, add on another $6,000 to $9,000 per acre. Many vineyard consultants advise a four to five acre plot to start out, selling off the grapes to other wineries and getting a feel for the business before expanding.

If you want to establish a bona fide winery, the cost of equipment is added on and your investment is up over several hundred thousand dollars in no time at all — and that is for a very small winery. You will have to start out with a minimum of 15 to 20 acres of plantable land to make it feasible. From a purely economical point of view, when the cost of marketing and distribution is added on, it does not make sense to invest in starting a winery. Fortunately, there is more to life than the short-term bottom line.

Q: What is the meaning of the word *cuvée* on Champagne bottles?

A: *Cuvée* (coo-vay) refers to a special or house blend of wines. In Champagne, France, the *cuvée* is a closely guarded secret by the great sparkling wine houses whose reputation and good name rely heavily on a consistent quality of wine expected by their customers. Although the term *cuvée* is most widely used in reference to the blending of sparkling wines, it is also used for premium blends of still wines as well. In either case, the *cuvée* could include the blending of wine batches from different barrels, vineyards, grapes and even from different years. The *cuvée* is the best example of the winemaker's personal style and individual taste, since he or she is able to blend any combination of available products to produce a unique signature wine. Currently, *cuvée*, or proprietary blended wine, is very popular in the United States marketplace. Some premium, Bordeaux-like, wine blends are marketed under the consortium trade name of Meritage.

Q: What is the purpose of either leaving or pruning branches near the bottom of the vine?

A: Generally vine branches closer to the ground are pruned away so the fruit buds will appear at the top of the vine and benefit from the sunshine while not being deprived of the vine's nutrients being absorbed by lower, non-bearing, sucker branches. Vineyard managers will leave bottom branches only when they are trying to renew the vine's trunk. When the bottom branches are trained upward on a support system they will begin to produce fruit as well.

Q: Do vineyard workers use a special tool or some sort of knife to cut off grape clusters?

A: Pickers do indeed use a knife during the harvesting of grapes. It is a very sharp knife with a hooked end, developed in Roman times and virtually unchanged. In recent years, various forms of strong shears also have been used. The vast majority of pickers, however, still prefer the ancient hooked knife. Technology does not always win out over tradition.

Q: I would like to start making wine at home. What else can I make wine from besides grapes?

A: Just about anything added to sugar, water and yeast will produce some sort of fermented liquid. It may taste a little strange, maybe even a lot strange. I have sampled maple leaf wine, potato wine, cranberry wine, even garlic and onion wine, which was great for cooking, but devastating on sensitive eyes and noses. Most grape growing regions are also a natural source for fruit and berry wines such as cherry, apple, peach, pear, blueberry, raspberry and plum. There are many more possibilities, like rhubarb, honey and dandelion wine. Recipes are available from your local winemaking shop or from books at the library or bookstore, or on the internet. Home winemaking can be very entertaining and rewarding, but I prefer to let my friendly, little old winemaker make my wine — it is *much* better.

Q: Do you have a recipe for making Concord grape wine?

A: Here is a basic recipe to start with. Mash a quantity of Concord grapes thoroughly and let them stand in a crock for a week or 10 days, stirring twice daily. Press off juice at the end of this time and place in a cask. Add an equal amount of water and 20 ounces of sugar per gallon of mixture if the juice is from Concord grapes. If from another variety, test it with the saccharometer before adding sugar. Stir thoroughly and allow to ferment through the bunghole of the carboy or barrel for 3 or 4 days before water-sealing. Rack off the wine into a clean carboy and bottle when clear. This wine is light and fairly dry. If a sweeter wine is preferred, add 2 pounds of sugar to each gallon of liquid. Store in a cool place after it is bottled, or the wine may work again. For more detailed instructions, contact your local home winemaking supplier or look under winemaking at the public library or on the internet.

Q: I continually read about the sudden rise in popularity of United States regional wines as well as wines from Italy, Australia, Chile, etc. What has taken these areas so long to finally decide to increase the quality of their products and suddenly be discovered?

A: The simple answer to your question is demand. As the public became more knowledgeable about food and wine they came to expect more for their money. Another reason is economics. As the prices rise in more popular areas, like France and Napa Valley, the customer turns to alternatives that meet their needs and fit their pocketbooks. The Italians, with their long history of winemaking as well as developed vineyards and distribution networks, were able to profit the most by quickly adapting to American consumer buying patterns. The other areas are also making great strides, but the process is slower because the vineyard's technology and marketing programs had to play "catch up" to operations that have been in existence for generations.

Q: What is meant by a wine's *terroir*?

A: There is no literal translation for the French word *terroir* (tair-wah). It is best to consider the term as a "descriptor" for the essence of a particular wine. *Terrior* usually refers to the unique aromas and flavors of a specific growing area or definitive appellation. For instance, the grape variety Cabernet Sauvignon is grown all over the world, but there are distinctive differences in the taste and bouquet of say a Stag's Leap Cabernet in California and the Cabernet Sauvignon of the Haut Medoc in Bordeaux or of the Hunter Valley in Australia. The differences in these wines result from the region's varying temperature, water, sunshine and soil conditions. Together, these growing elements make up a wine's *terrior*.

Q: What part does yeast play in the process?

A: The English word yeast comes from either the Greek *zestos* or Sanskrit *yasyati*, both meaning to "boil" without heat, referring to a yeast-induced fermentation. Next to the grape, yeast is the most important element in wine, for this microscopic plant organism is the sole producer of fermentation that changes grape juice into wine. Yeasts "eat" or metabolize the natural sugars in the grapes, producing in equal amounts, alcohol and an inert gas called carbon dioxide that accounts for the bubbles in sparkling wines like Champagne. Although "wild" yeasts occur naturally on grapes, they are sometimes unpredictable in winemaking. Over the years, researchers have isolated a number of cultured strains in a pure form that add subtle flavor nuances and other desirable attributes to the finished wine.

Q: About fifteen years ago I made some grape wine. It has been sitting down in my basement all this time and I wonder if it is any good to drink?

A: It is quite possible that the wine is just fine. There is only one way to find out and that is to open it up. Your nose will be the first indication as to whether you wish to taste it or not. If it smells bad, it will more than likely taste the same way. It would be kind of fun just to see how well you did fifteen years ago.

Q: Why do wine bottles have corks?

A: The cork is an organic closure that permits the interchange of air with wine at a rate that allows wine to mature. Wine bottles with corks should be stored either upside down or on their sides, so the cork remains moist and does not dry out and shrink. If this happens, the closure is no longer tight and excessive aeration takes place. Too much exposure to air may cause wine to darken and lose some of its bouquet. The taste will begin to gradually change. The extreme end product of this natural process is vinegar.

Q: If a wine cork that has gone bad imparts an unpalatable taste to the wine, then why even use a cork in the first place?

A: Cork is used as a wine closure because it is a natural product, from the bark of a cork oak tree. Cork has elastic properties that enable it to conform to irregularities in the neck of a bottle for a better seal. Also, according to some schools of thought, cork aids in the development of a wine aging in a bottle by imparting a minute amount of cork flavor. The intensity of this flavor naturally increases the longer the wine is in the bottle. It is almost imperceptible in the first few years of aging, as it is developed very slowly. This is based on the assumption that the cork and the wine are in constant contact. The alcohol in the wine slowly extracts the flavor from the cork. These are the reasons why a cork is the traditional closure. It was also believed, that air was transmitted through the cork to the wine, enhancing its ability to age. This theory was recently questioned by scientists at the University of California at Davis. With elaborate testing, scientists refuted this premise. Research never ends in the wine industry.

Q: What happens if a winery or farmer plants a particular variety of grapevine and after the four or five years it takes to mature, the variety is out of favor with the consumer?

A: You have probably already guessed the obvious answer. They must pull up the vineyard and replant it or let it go wild on its own. It is extremely costly to tear out and replant vineyards, so much care and research goes into the decision of what and how much to plant. For the most part, unless a farmer took a big gamble on predicting the public's wine taste, most pull-ups of vineyards are minimal. They do happen, however, on a regular basis with wineries who constantly adjust to the changing palate of the American consumer.

Q: Do all wineries grow their own grapes?

A: Not necessarily. Many of the wineries do plant vineyards for their wine, but often needing more grapes than they can grow, they buy from independent growers. Larger wineries, as a matter of regular business, contract with growers to supply all the grapes that will be needed to meet projected production needs. The winemaker works very closely with these growers to ensure they meet specified standards of production in order to achieve the quality of wine desired. Since the contracts between the winery and the grower are very specific about the type of grape, the production yield and quality control, the wineries know exactly what they will be working with, provided Mother Nature cooperates.

Q: Why do some wine labels carry the name of the grape and some have a name that seems to be made up?

A: When a wine is made from at least 75% of a particular grape variety it is called a varietal wine and the name of the grape may be used on the label. Some typical examples of varietal wines are Cabernet Sauvignon, Chardonnay, Merlot, Vidal Blanc, Chancellor and Riesling, to name a few. The tendency of late is to blend a mixture of compatible varieties in order to give the winemaker an opportunity to use the best grapes available and to exercise some creative winemaking to produce the best possible product and value. Called proprietary wines, they are a blend of wines developed by the proprietor and carry such creative private label names as Trillium, Jester's Blush, Lilac Hill or simply, White Table Wine. Some people have the mistaken perception that varietal wines are the best quality wines. That is not always the case. Mouton Cadet, many French chateau bottled wines and most all Champagnes are just a few examples of famous blended proprietary wines of top quality.

Q: If frost in the spring and rain at harvest are the villains of the vineyards, does that mean the summer is easy going for grape growers?

A: Not by a long shot! Although uncontrollable frost and rain are more critical to the outcome of the total production, there is still the constant battle with insects and fungus diseases, such as mites and mildew. Growers have learned to control these problems with environmentally safe sprays, but birds are nature's biggest pest to ripening grape bunches. Great clouds of birds have been know to assault a vineyard and eat it clean of grapes within a few hours. Growers have tried nets, shotguns, recorded sounds and even recordings on timers that go off with a variety of blaring sound effects to scare the birds. Nothing works effectively for long, but fortunately the bird problem is not widespread nor is it consistent from year to year. One Michigan winemaker who had a particular grape variety completely wiped out released a fully packaged bottle minus the wine and called the product, "The Wine the Birds Ate." Wine critics considered it "a bit lacking in body."

Q: What are organic wines?

A: As most any winemaker will tell you, "everything starts in the vineyards." Currently, much research is being done on "organic farming" — a system of farming eliminating the use of chemical fertilizers, pesticides, herbicides or fungicides. Obviously, with today's economic demands on crop yields it becomes a very difficult task to control insects, pests and plant disease without the careful use of agricultural chemicals. Some of the new techniques include recycling grape pomace (the by-product of the winemaking process) as a natural fertilizer in the vineyards, planting cover crops of native weeds and grasses in the vineyards to replenish natural organic material in the soil and the placement of certain natural predators to insects and vine-damaging rodents. It is now a common site in many California vineyards to see manmade shelters and perches for hawks, owls and bats — such are the lengths we go for a bottle of wine.

Q: While visiting California wineries I noticed many vineyards had roses planted at the end of rows. Besides being attractive, is there any practical reason for the plants?

A: In years gone by, rose bushes were planted in vineyards because the rose plants were sensitive to some of the diseases and insects that infect vines - mildew, bugs, etc. If the rose bush showed stress, the farmer would do a careful evaluation of the vineyard and take whatever preventative measures were needed. Nowadays, due to advanced technological procedures, most wineries diligently monitor the soil and health of the plants on a daily basis, and do not need those "centurion" roses. For the most part, the roses add beauty to the landscape and some wineries will plant red roses to identify the red grape varieties and white flowers for the rows of white grapes.

Wine and Food

After bread comes wine, the second nutriment
given by the Creator to sustain life and the first
to be famed for its excellence.

OLIVER DESERRES

•

In most European households,
a bottle of wine on the table is more important
than the salt and pepper shakers.

JOE BORRELLO

Q: Which wines are proper with which foods?

A: The word "proper" creates a misconception about wine for many people. If you like the wine, it is proper. There are no laws that must be obeyed. Having said that, however, sweet wines have a tendency to numb the taste buds, so keep that in mind when you are trying to match food with wine. Dry or semi-dry wines would be preferable with meals. Generally speaking, this will allow you to maximize the pleasure of both the wine and the flavor of the food. Experiment on your own with different foods and sauces, you will be amazed at the different taste sensations that can be created by changing the wine companion. To get you started, here are some suggested match-ups from Tasters Guild International, a national food and wine appreciation society.

FOOD	SUGGESTED WINES
Appetizers	
Dips & canapés	Riesling, Sauvignon Blanc, Dry Chenin Blanc
Paté	Chilled Dry Sherry, Alsatian Pinot Gris, Fumé Blanc
Shellfish	Chablis, Chardonnay, Champagne, Muscadet
Caviar	Brut Champagne (The classic is iced Vodka)
Fish	
Fresh water fish	Chilean Chardonnay, Pinot Gris/Grigio, Sauvignon Blanc
Seafood (salmon, tuna, etc.)	Premium Chardonnay, French White Burgundies
Grilled or highly seasoned	Reserve Chardonnay, Pinot Noir, Côtes du Rhône
Poultry	
Barbecue chicken	Dry Rosé, Pinot Noir, Gamay Beaujolais
Roasted chicken or turkey	Riesling, Chenin Blanc, Blush/Rosé, Beaujolais

Poultry (cont.)

For basting chicken or ham	Gewürztraminer, Cherry Wine, other fruit wines
For marinating chicken	Sauvignon Blanc, Pinot Grigio, Dry Riesling
Roasted game birds	Syrah, Pinot Noir, Zinfandel
Duck or goose	Mature Cabernet Sauvignon, Chateauneuf du Pape

Meats

Game meat	Pinot Noir, Shiraz/Syrah, Barolo, Barbaresco
Grilled beef steak	Shiraz/Syrah, Malbec, Cabernet Sauvignon, Rhônes, Petite Sirah
For marinating beef	An inexpensive dry, red wine
Roast beef	Merlot, Chambourcin, Pinot Noir
Stew or casserole	Zinfandel, Shiraz/Syrah, Burgundy-style wines
Broiled veal	Valpolicella, Beaujolais, Pinot Noir, Merlot
Sautéed veal	Vouvray, Pinot Gris/Grigio, Dry Riesling
Sausage or cold cuts	Riesling, Generic White Wine, Blush/Rosé, Malbec
Pork roast or chops	Chilean Merlot, French Beaujolais, Chardonnay
Barbecue ribs	Dry Rosé, Pinot Noir, Gamay Beaujolais
Ham	Gewürztraminer, Vouvray, Riesling, Blush wines
Lamb	Cabernet Sauvignon, Chancellor, Spanish Rioja
Venison	Rhône, Bordeaux, California Cabs

Miscellaneous

Grilled or sautéed vegetables	Valpolicella, Merlot, Shiraz/Syrah
Pasta with white sauce	Pinot Gris/Grigio, Soave, Frascatti, Gavi
Pasta with tomato base	Zinfandel or any Italian red wine

Desserts

Apple pie or cobbler	German or Loire Valley sweet whites, Ice Wine
Chocolate	Port, Zinfandel, Australian Shiraz
Fresh Fruit	Late Harvest white wines, Sauternes, Muscato

Q: Does the guideline, "white wine with white meat and red wine with red meat" still apply?

A: It is still a pretty good rule of thumb, but today's cooking is much more sophisticated and complex. Many of the old cooking "laws" are being thrown out the window by enterprising young chefs who are constantly looking for new and different approaches to making food more interesting. Today, fish and chicken dishes are being served with red sauces and beef with cream and herb sauces. Now, what wine do we serve? The key is to try different combinations of food and wine. There really is no set rule and it is quite acceptable to have a light red wine with a spicy Cajun seafood dish or a hearty white wine with a beef entrée. There are still flavor combinations of food that are more naturally complemented by certain wines, but the main objective is to enjoy what you are eating and the wine you are drinking. Experiment and let your palate be your guide.

Q: Do you have any useful tips on cooking with wine?

A: It seems that Americans have discovered only recently the joy of cooking with wine and the difference it can make in a very wide variety of foods. Many people have not tried cooking with wine because they are unsure of its use as a seasoning agent and how much is enough. It is difficult to overdo wine — the more you add, the more flavor you will achieve. It all depends upon how juicy or liquid you want the finished dish.

- Using wine as a substitute for a portion of liquid in almost any recipe will add enormously to the flavor and richness of the dish.
- First try a small amount of wine, so the flavors will blend subtly and not become overpowering.
- Wine gives flavor to some dishes that would be bland or flat without it.
- The flavor of wine in cooking is due to the nature of the wine and not the alcohol.
- During cooking, most of the alcohol evaporates (alcohol boils and evaporates at 172°F., the temperature at which water only simmers) and little alcohol is present in the finished dish.
- For meat dishes calling for wine, first heat the wine (do not boil or you will lose the flavor).

- Adding cold wine tends to make meat tough, while warm wine helps tenderize it.
- For fish and chicken, use a dry or semi-dry white wine.
- Dry red wines have a better chemistry with heavier red meats.
- One thing to keep in mind is that when wine is first added to a dish it imparts little flavor. Therefore, it is best to let it cook for a few minutes before tasting. You will be astonished at the difference even 5 minutes makes.

Q: Which wines are better than others for cooking?

A: Not the ones that are labeled "Cooking Wine." Rule Number One: "If it isn't good enough to drink, it isn't good enough to cook with." So-called "Cooking Wine" usually has a lot of sodium added. This does not mean, however, that you should use your best wine. A well-made, medium body and inexpensive (under $10) wine is just fine. I prefer Sauvignon Blanc as a white wine for sautéing, marinating and use in sauces for seafood, chicken and veal. I have been very pleased with the results of using Gallo Hearty Burgundy as a red wine for preparation of meat and meat based sauces. It is best to stay away from wines that are heavily flavored with oak. These wines have a tendency to give off a bitter taste in sauces. I have found that generic, blended red wines give better cooking results than do varietal wines such as Cabernet Sauvignon and Zinfandel.

Q: Should I use wine in recipes that don't call for it?

A: Use wine as a substitute for a portion of liquid in almost any recipe. Experiment with a small amount of wine, so the flavors will blend subtly and not become overpowering. If you enjoy a more pronounced wine flavor, add more wine to suit your taste just before the dish is served. In the process of cooking with wine, the alcohol evaporates, along with the calories. Never boil wine, however, or you will also boil out the flavor.

Q: How do you create the flambé in table side cooking?

A: First you must use a flammable liquor like brandy or 151-proof rum. The trick to setting liquor aflame in drinks or food dishes is to pre-warm the glass or cooking vessel, and the liquor. Pour the recipe amount (reserving a spoonful) of liquor on top of the rest of the ingredients, being careful not to stir it into the mixture. Preheat the reserved spoonful of liquor, light it, then pour it into the remaining liquor to be set aflame.

Q: What foods, other than desserts, would you recommend with French Sauternes?

A: Sauternes and the other sweet white wines of Bordeaux, such as Barsac, are frequently served only as dessert wines in this country. While visiting Chateau Suduiraut, a while back, I was served a number of different vintages of the chateau's delicious Sauternes throughout a luncheon buffet of fresh shellfish. The combination was marvelous. Sauternes also bring out the sweetness of lobster and are natural partners for rich patés, melon or sweetbreads in cream sauces. After a meal, Sauternes are excellent with fruit, Roquefort cheese or simply served by themselves, cold, but not iced.

Q: What wines would you suggest with appetizers before a dinner party?

A: Appetizers and *aperitif* wines are meant to tease and stimulate the palate before a meal. They should be dry or off-dry. Sweet wines have a tendency to numb the taste buds and overpower food flavors. Light bodied, semi-dry white wines like Riesling, Chenin Blanc, Vouvray and some of the new proprietary wines have refreshing tastes and sensations that make them easy to sip before dinner. They are especially appealing to guests who do not normally drink wine and are appreciated by those who have cut back on the consumption of hard liquor. The slight residual sugar in these wines will go well with appetizers that are smoked, salty or spiced. Dry sparkling and still white wines tend to cleanse and sharpen one's palate. Pinot Gris/Grigio, Grand Cru Chablis, Sauvignon Blanc, Frascati and Champagne combine very well with the delicate flavors of a wide variety of shellfish and seafood *hors d'oeuvres*. A combination of complementing flavors have a tendency to stimulate your guests' appetites.

Q: Is it true no wine goes well with chocolate?

A: It is true that some wine experts are reluctant to recommend any particular wine with chocolate because it takes so many forms and usually overpowers the flavor of most wines. Sweet German-style wines and Sauternes are popular choices with chocolate desserts as are many sparkling wines such as Asti Spumante and semi-dry Champagnes. Some adventurous souls enjoy the flavor combination of a young and hearty, full-bodied Cabernet Sauvignon, Zinfandel or Shiraz with chocolate. Raspberry or cherry wine complements chocolate very nicely as well, either by itself or added into a sparkling wine for a more elegant and tasty presentation.

Q: I am a waiter in a rather expensive restaurant and have bitten my tongue when a guest orders a wine that does not go with the entrée. Should I say something, or is "the customer always right?"

A: This is a very touchy situation and requires a bit of diplomacy on your part. First and foremost, you do not want to embarrass the customer in front of other guests. On the other hand, you would be doing a service to the guests if you were to steer the client away from a bad choice. The easiest method would be to shift the blame, by saying, "I served this wine the other day and it was a bit disappointing," or "the chef's treatment of this dish changes the traditional match up with this wine." Use your own judgment as to how well informed the customer is with the selection and always be ready to suggest an appropriate alternative. Always remain polite and never challenge the guest's final decision, no matter how wrong you may think he or she is.

Q: Which orange liqueur would you suggest?

A: The most popular orange base liqueurs are Triple Sec, Curacao, Cointreau and Grand Marnier. All are used quite successfully in the preparation of many fine desserts. Triple Sec is the least expensive of the four and is frequently used by restaurants and bakeshops.

Q: What is Amaretto? Why does it have a unique almond flavor?

A: Amaretto is a liqueur made from the almonds of apricots and seeped in *acquavite,* a fusion of alcohol. The most popular and possibly the best quality Amaretto comes from Italy. The aromatic apricot-almond liqueur dispenses a distinctive bouquet and flavor that has made Amaretto one of the best selling cordials in the world. Chefs and bakers have also found that the liqueur is an excellent flavor ingredient, particularly in desserts.

Q: I consider myself a good cook, but I would like to know more about cooking with wine. Any suggestions, short of culinary school?

A: Unfortunately, many household cooks have the notion that cooking with wine takes some special culinary training, wine expertise or exotic recipes. Nothing is further from the truth. If a recipe calls for water, add a little wine for a more fragrant and better tasting dish. White wine added to cream sauces gives an elegant smoothness and aroma to the dish. Also add white wine to a seafood dish or marinade and you will find the wine breaks down the odorous fish oils, just as lemon juice and vinegar do.

Q: Would you recommend using Champagne in cooking?

A: The high acid content of sparkling wines and their bubbles add a real tantalizing tanginess to light cream sauces. While Champagne-style wines are generally considered festive beverages only, they are also excellent wines for cooking delicate sauce dishes. It may seem a bit extravagant to cook with Champagne, but use only about half as much "bubbly" as you would a still table wine, due to the higher acidity. Sparkling wines will add a little zest to your recipes, but they will retain the bubbles for only a short time. You would be better served if you put it in your sauce just before serving the dish.

Q: Do you have any recipes for cooking with Champagne?

A: From the recipes of Perrier-Jouet comes this little salmon treat. Use thick salmon steaks. Butter an ovenproof dish and line it with finely chopped shallots and a mixture of diced vegetables. Lay the salmon steaks on the bed and moisten halfway with an equal mixture of fish stock and Champagne. Bake in a preheated oven at 425° F for about 20-25 minutes. Drain and keep warm. Strain the cooking juices and add some cream (about half as much as the juices), then reduce by half. Adjust seasoning to taste. Add a large piece of butter cut into small pieces and beat. Coat the steaks with this sauce and serve.

Q: What wine would you recommend for Chinese wok cooking?

A: It does not matter what you cook in, rather it is what you cook. The whole idea of cooking with wine is marrying the flavors of the food with the wine. If you are stir-frying vegetables or chicken, use dry or semi-dry white wines that will complement, not overpower the subtle flavors with which you are working. If meat and strong seasonings like garlic are being used, then try dry red wines that will stand up to and enhance the heavier flavors. Exploring different food and wine flavors is the real "joy of cooking."

Q: How do you make the wine vinegar starter known as the "mother?"

A: Time and chance are crucial ingredients in creating the "mother" starter for wine vinegar. Start with apple juice without preservatives, or better yet, fresh unfiltered apple cider. Apple juice reacts very favorably to the correct bacteria needed to start the natural process. Pour the juice into 3 or 4 separate containers and stretch cheese cloth over the tops to keep out fruit flies. Let the containers set for a few months and, as the juice is inoculated naturally by bacteria in the air, it will turn sour. Test the containers for the desired taste and select one to place into a batch of wine to begin the vinegar process. Since there are different types of bacteria in the air, you may well get different tastes from your starter batches. The starter routine can be speeded up if you can find an unpasteurized and unfiltered wine vinegar to place in the apple juice. Conditions are also better for the proper bacteria in August or September during fruit harvest time.

Q: What wine do you suggest for serving with pork tenderloin?

A: A current popular grape variety is Pinot Gris (from Alsace, Oregon or the Great Lakes Region), also known as Pinot Grigio in Italy. The wine is light, dry and has an agreeable fruit flavor that will complement your pork tenderloin nicely (especially if the meat is grilled). If you prefer red wines, stay with the lighter styles, like the blush or rosé wines. White Zinfandel is a favorite for many and is a neutral wine for a large group with divergent tastes, but do not get it too sweet. For the turkey traditionalist, Beaujolais Nouveau is the perfect all-around wine for the winter holidays. If you prefer a white wine, select a dry or semi-dry Riesling to grace your table and please your guests. All of the above wines should be served slightly chilled.

Q: What wine would you suggest with spicy ethnic foods?

A: Would you believe Champagne? One of the best buffers against the predominate flavors of Tex-Mex, Indian and Hunan foods is the refreshing sensation of sparkling bubbles consuming the heat in your mouth. The beauty is that the heat of the spices are so dominate that elegant French Champagne would be a waste of money, so a well-chilled bottle of just about any type of inexpensive sparkling wine will add a special touch to a festive occasion.

Q: Why is the sense of smell the most important element in tasting wine?

A: The greatest proportion (about 80%) of what we normally consider to be taste or flavor is actually smell. When wine is sniffed, the olfactory or odor-sensitive portion of the nose is opened and collects information that is transmitted to the brain. Additional information reaches the olfactory region when one tastes the wine and exhales through the nose. This aerates and warms the wine sufficiently to release more volatile components. The smell combined with the tongue's contribution of the taste sensations, sweet, sour, salty and bitter, all add to the full pleasure of the wine. As an experiment, hold your nose as you sip a little wine and notice how much flavor is missing compared to using both senses. The sensation is similar to trying to taste food with a cold.

Q: How much value should I put in a wine steward's suggestion of wine to go with my meal? Are they just pushing products they want to get rid of?

A: I suppose that could be true in some isolated cases, but I have found the wine steward's suggestion is quite often better than my own selection. Remember, wine stewards work with the same wines and menu everyday. They know which wines from their cellar are ready to drink, which are the better values and which would best accompany your meal. If the wine steward is good at his or her job, the wine list has been selected to complement the chef's creations, and I am not about to challenge the recommendation. At least, not until I taste it with the food.

Q: Which wine would you suggest when serving ham?

A: There are many alternatives, but none that are perfect all the time. Ham may make a chef fantasize over exotic and creative recipes, but it can create nightmares trying to pick a wine to go with the infinite number of sweet glazes and preparations for this versatile meat. The common sweet and sour presentation calls for a wine with some sweetness or carbonation — a good reason to try a sparkling wine. Dry white wines often taste drier and red wines will taste slightly bitter and astringent with ham. For the most part, off-dry wines from grape varieties like Riesling, Vidal Blanc, Gewürztraminer or one of the many blush wines would be the best partners for ham. The wine you choose should depend upon the seasonings used in the preparation. Remember, the sweeter the sauces and glazes, the more they will mask the fruit flavors of any wine which is served.

Q: What does wine add to a sauce and how do I use it?

A: Wine is a seasoning, like herbs or spices, only in liquid form. It accents and improves natural food flavors and adds a certain flair to ordinary cooking, yet it is easy to use. Instead of adding water, which is tasteless, to your recipe, substitute some wine. You will discover a much more fragrant and better-tasting dish. Add the wine near the end of your cooking for more intense flavoring.

Q: Does wine make a good marinade?

A: Meat may be tenderized and its flavor enhanced by marinating in red wine for an hour or two. You will also find adding white wine to a seafood marinade will break down the odorous fish oils, just as lemon juice and vinegar do. Marinating should be done in glass, porcelain or materials other than aluminum, which has a tendency to give an off-flavor to a wine marinade. Many semi-sweet wines and champagnes are particularly pleasing as a marinade for fresh fruit served in a wine glass, plus they add an elegant touch to your table setting.

Q: What wine would you recommend serving with rack of lamb?

A: The classic wine would be Cabernet Sauvignon or Merlot, but Zinfandel and Chancellor could be just as pleasing. The reason these wines marry so well with lamb is because the meat's slight oiliness softens the wine tannin and enables the wine's subtler flavors to develop and stand out.

Q: What wines are best with game birds?

A: Quail and game hens have a sweet meat that affects other flavors. For example, grilled quail with herbs will have a smoky character that would be compatible with a dry Sauvignon Blanc or Burgundian Chardonnay. The same bird roasted and served with a wine sauce might better match a Syrah or Zinfandel. Squab, a dark meat, stronger-flavored bird, usually needs a fruity, acidic red or white wine that can handle the distinctive gamey taste. Marinating any of these birds in a fruit or berry wine presents a fruitier flavor that would be delicious with a Pinot Noir or Gamay Beaujolais. Selecting a wine, however, will be influenced by the cooking method, sauces, stuffings and marinades that are used with any of these dishes.

Q: Is it me, or does wine not go very well with the salad course? I seem to have a real hard time enjoying wine with salads containing vinaigrette dressings.

A: Although drinking wine with a vinaigrette salad dressing may be undesirable, many cooks prefer vinegar made from wine. Strange as it may sound, wine vinegar does have a decidedly less harsh taste than cider varieties. Thus, it intermingles with and adds complexity rather than dominating other food flavors and smells. Wine vinegars can be found as red, white, herbed and spiced. They add a nice touch to a tasty crisp salad.

Q: Are there foods that may also not be compatible with wine?

A: Most foods go well with wine, but there are some flavors which should be worked around or toned down when wine is an important part of the meal. Included in these are curry, horseradish, hot peppers, citrus rinds, excessive fats and oils and heavy chocolate. In addition, one surprising food is asparagus. It can dull your palate, so it is better served as a separate course without wine.

Q: Could you make some suggestions about which wines to serve with cheese?

A: Flavored cream cheeses match well with fruit (other than grape) wines. Chardonnay is a hit with almost any mild, soft cheese offered as an appetizer. White Cheddar and Merlot are natural partners, as are Brie and Pinot Gris. Try Pinot Noir or Zinfandel with the popular goat cheeses and Chianti Classico Riserva or Cabernet Sauvignon with fresh Parmesan or Asiago. How about pairing a blue cheese with either Cream Sherry or a Late Harvest Riesling for dessert? Of course, port and aged cheddar or Stilton are classic matches. You should have no problem finding either the cheeses or the wines at the specialty food and wine section of the supermarket. Wine and cheese are natural food partners and have a lot in common. Both are products of the fermentation process and offer a wide variety of styles; from simple and mild to complex and aged. Wine and cheese is one of the most popular and appealing party themes for contemporary entertaining.

Q: What is the classic food match-up with Champagne?

A: Although a lot of a people would like to believe that a "touch of the bubbly" complements most any meal or course, I have found that sparkling wines are always at their finest as the *aperitif* with *hors d'oeuvres* and then again with dessert. In my opinion, the bubbles distract the taste buds from the more complex flavors of a main entrée. An exception to this would be brunch, where Champagne seems to have a very complementary effect on the combination of foods and it does add to an atmosphere of "casual decadence."

Q: I have a friend coming to visit from South America and he is bringing some Venezuelan Beaver cheese. What kind of wine do I serve with it?

A: This was an actual question I received on a phone-in radio program on location at a local wine bar. After looking around the crowded room for some help and watching my friends all turn their backs to me, giggling uncontrollably, I got the impression I was being set-up. However, it was live radio and the caller was still on the line. "Well," I stammered, "I'm not very familiar with Venezuelan Beaver cheese, but I'll suggest this: If you can smell him coming up the walk, serve a hearty red." We quickly cut to commercials as my so-called friends assisted each other up off the floor.

Recipes with Wine

The wine I loved deeply. The dice I love dearly.

KING LEAR,
WILLIAM SHAKESPEARE

•

A recipe without wine is like passing the dice
at the craps table — you miss all the fun.

JOE BORRELLO

Q: What is a good wine recipe for venison and other meats?

A: Here are several.

Venison Swiss Steak

A version of Venison Swiss Steak from the folks at Good Harbor Vineyards in Lake Leelanau, Michigan.

Serving Size: 6

2 pounds venison steak cut into serving pieces
1 package dry onion soup mix
2 cups dry red wine
2 cups water
16 ounces canned tomato sauce
2 bay leaves
2 teaspoons Italian seasonings (oregano, basil, etc.)
flour
vegetable oil
salt and pepper

Cover meat with flour, then brown on both sides in oil. Drain. Combine wine, tomato sauce, soup mix, water and seasonings, then pour over meat. Bring mixture to a boil, reduce heat, and simmer covered until tender, about 2 hours. Add more wine and water if sauce gets too thick. May cook for two hours in a crock pot if desired.

Per serving: 375 Calories; 10g Fat (27% calories from fat); 47g Protein; 11g Carbohydrate; 125mg Cholesterol; 1198mg Sodium

Suggested Wine: *Barolo or vintage Red Burgundy*

Pork Chops with Pear Purée and Blueberries

From the magazine *La Cucina Italiana* comes this dish with a sauce that is traditionally paired with game in Northern Italy, but is exceptionally delicious with pork chops.

Serving Size: 4

3 medium pears, peeled, cored and sliced
3 tablespoons unsalted butter
3/4 cup dry white wine
1 pound pork chops, (4 4-ounces each)
1 cup flour
2 tablespoons blueberries, fresh or frozen
salt to taste
fresh ground black pepper

Sauté the pears in a 12" skillet with a tablespoon of the butter for 5 minutes over medium-high heat. Add 1/2 cup of wine; cook 10 minutes. Purée in a blender.

Meanwhile, dredge the pork chops in flour, and shake off excess. Heat the remaining butter in another 12" skillet. Add the pork, cook until golden brown on both sides, turning once, 4 minutes per side. Add the remaining wine, blueberries, salt and pepper. Cook 2 minutes.

Transfer the pork to 4 plates; mound the pear purée next to it. Crush half of the blueberries in the skillet and spoon the resulting mixture over the pork. Serve immediately.

Per serving: 499 Calories; 21g Fat (40% calories from fat); 22g Protein; 50g Carbohydrate; 80mg Cholesterol; 49mg Sodium

Suggested Wine: *Chilled dry rosé or Gamay Beaujolais*

Meat Marinade

Here is a meat marinade that works well with beef or game.

1/8 cup olive oil
2 tablespoons Balsamic vinegar
3 cloves garlic, minced
1/4 cup green onions, chopped
1/4 cup dry red wine

   Mix all ingredients together. Pour over meat and marinate in refrigerator overnight. Turn meat at least once. Marinate in glass bowl or heavy plastic freezer bag.

Per serving: 76 Calories; 7g Fat (88% calories from fat); 0g Protein; 2g Carbohydrate; 0mg Cholesterol; 10mg Sodium

NOTES

_____

_____

_____

_____

_____

_____

_____

_____

_____

Molasses, Portobella Mushroom & Black Pepper Beef Marinade

A Southwestern twist to the preparation of beef or game.

Serving Size: 4

1 cup molasses
2/3 cup dry red wine
2 tablespoons balsamic vinegar
2 tablespoons black pepper, freshly ground
2 cloves garlic, finely chopped
1 bunch green onions, finely chopped
2 teaspoons fresh ginger, finely grated
1 teaspoon fresh thyme, finely chopped
crushed red pepper to taste
salt to taste
3 ounces grilled portobella mushrooms, coarsely chopped

Place sirloin, tenderloin of beef or venison in a glass dish. In a small bowl, combine molasses, wine, balsamic vinegar, black pepper, garlic, onions, ginger, thyme and pepper flakes. When well-blended, pour over meat. Cover. Refrigerate, allowing meat to marinate for 24 hours (at least overnight), turning occasionally.

Grill mushrooms, chop and set aside until ready to cook meat.

Salt meat and grill (or pan fry slices in 2 tablespoons of vegetable oil) at medium high heat.

While meat is cooking, pour marinade juice and chopped mushrooms in a separate fry pan. Reduce liquid by half.

When ready to serve meat, present the compote on the side or on top of sliced meat.

Note: If there is any meat left over, slice it up and wrap with flour tortilla. Cut into bite size pieces and serve as an *hors d'oeuvre*.

Per serving (without meat): 270 Calories; less than one gram Fat (1% calories from fat); 1g Protein; 63g Carbohydrate; 0mg Cholesterol; 59mg Sodium

Suggested Wine: *California Cabernet Sauvignon or Australian Shiraz.*

Steak Au Poivre with Cognac Cream Sauce

As long as we are on the subject of meat, here is a steak recipe that is outstanding for impressing dinner guests, as long as they are not watching their waist lines.

Serving Size: 4

SAUCE:
4 tablespoons unsalted butter
1 medium minced shallot
3/4 cup nonfat beef broth
1/4 cup nonfat chicken broth
1/4 cup heavy cream
1/4 cup Cognac
1 tablespoon brandy
1 teaspoon lemon juice
sea salt

STEAKS:
4 6-ounce sirloin steaks, trimmed, 3/4 to 1 inch thick
1 tablespoon coarse, ground, multicolor peppercorns

Heat 1 tablespoon butter in 12-inch heavy-bottomed skillet over medium heat; when foaming subsides, add shallot and cook, stirring occasionally, until softened, about 2 minutes. Add beef and chicken broths, increase heat to high, and boil until reduced to about 1/2 cup, about 8 minutes. Place reduced broth mixture in a bowl and set aside. Rinse and wipe out skillet.

Meanwhile, sprinkle both sides of steaks with salt; rub one side of each steak with 1 teaspoon crushed peppercorns, and, using fingers, press peppercorns into steaks to make them adhere. Place now-empty skillet over medium heat until hot, about 4 minutes. Lay steak unpeppered side down in hot skillet, increase heat to medium-high, firmly press down on steaks with bottom of cake pan, and cook steaks without moving them until well-browned, about 6 minutes. Using tongs, flip steaks, firmly press down on steaks with bottom of cake pan, and cook on peppered side, about 3 minutes longer for rare, about 4 minutes longer for medium rare. Transfer steaks to large plate and tent loosely with foil to keep warm. Pour reduced broth, cream and 1/4 cup cognac into now-empty skillet; increase heat to high and bring to boil, scraping pan bottom with wooden spoon to loosen browned bits. Simmer until deep golden brown and thick enough to heavily coat back of metal tablespoon or soup spoon, about 5 minutes. Take off heat, whisk in remaining 3 tablespoons butter, remaining 1 tablespoon cognac, lemon juice or vinegar and any accumulated meat juices. Adjust seasonings with salt.

Set steaks on individual dinner plates, spoon portion of sauce over steaks and serve immediately.

Note: Make sure the peppercorns are coarsely ground - that's the secret.

Per serving: 443 Calories; 27g Fat (60% calories from fat); 38g Protein; 2g Carbohydrate; 157mg Cholesterol; 271mg Sodium

Suggested Wine: *Syrah or Petite Sirah*

NOTES

_____

_____

_____

_____

_____

_____

_____

_____

Korean Grilled Beef

A real Asian treat!

Serving Size: 4

4 6-ounce sirloin steaks, trimmed, 3/4 to 1-inch thick
1 tablespoon toasted sesame seeds, crushed
4 cloves garlic, chopped
2 tablespoons soy sauce
1/4 cup vegetable oil
1/4 cup olive oil
8 drops Chinese hot oil
1/8 cup Balsamic vinegar
1 teaspoon sugar
1/4 cup cream-style sherry

Toast sesame seeds and crush. Mix all ingredients together and pour over meat in a heavy-duty plastic bag or glass casserole. Place in refrigerator overnight.

Grill meat, then cut into 1 1/2 inch serving strips.

Reduce leftover marinade in saucepan by half and drizzle sauce on meat strips. Serve with rice and grilled vegetables.

Per serving: 519 Calories; 37g Fat (66% calories from fat); 37g Protein; 5g Carbohydrate; 104mg Cholesterol; 615mg Sodium

Suggested Wine: *Zinfandel*

Polish Kielbasa

How about another ethic treat — Polish Kielbasa — always a hit around the holidays, from the Polish side of our family.

Serving Size: 10

3 pounds ground pork butt or loin
1 tablespoon fresh garlic finely chopped
1 teaspoon fresh ground pepper
3 teaspoons salt
2 teaspoons mustard seed
1 tablespoon marjoram
1 cup white wine

Mix all ingredients and let marinate, covered, in the refrigerator overnight.

Stuff into casings (available from your butcher) and boil in beer (or water) for 25-30 minutes.

Serve with fresh horseradish.

Fry the leftovers and serve with toast and eggs for breakfast.

Per serving: 410 Calories; 29g Fat (64% calories from fat); 35g Protein; 1g Carbohydrate; 128mg Cholesterol; 740mg Sodium

NOTES

_____

_____

_____

_____

_____

Greek Cocktail Meatballs

A Greek chef thought I would enjoy this appetizer recipe, and I did.

Serving Size: 12

1 pound ground beef
1/2 pound ground lamb
1 medium onion, finely chopped
1 clove minced garlic
2 large eggs
4 tablespoons fresh parsley, finely chopped
1/4 teaspoon dried oregano
1/4 teaspoon dried mint leaves
1/2 teaspoon dried basil
3 tablespoons olive oil
1/2 cup grated Parmesan cheese
1/2 cup white wine
10 slices bread soaked in water
2 tablespoons Ouzo (a Greek distilled drink)

Squeeze water soaked bread to remove liquid.

Fill a large baking dish with three tablespoons of olive oil.

Combine all the ingredients, omitting a quarter cup of wine. Knead meatballs well, form small bite size balls and put in baking dish. Bake in hot oven at 475°F for about 20-30 minutes.

Pour the quarter cup of leftover wine in the baking dish, turn the meatballs and bake for an additional 10 minutes.

Keep meatballs warm in a chafing dish until ready to serve.

Per serving; 303 Calories; 20g Fat (64% calories from fat); 14g Protein; 12g Carbohydrate; 79mg Cholesterol; 227mg Sodium

Suggested Wine: *Chardonnay*

Pork Loin Barbecue

Great for shredded pork sandwiches.

Serving Size: 6

3 pounds pork loin, boned
2 tablespoons soy sauce
1 tablespoon sesame oil
1/2 cup dry white wine
3 cloves chopped garlic
salt and pepper to taste
1 can chicken broth

Fold pork loin and all ingredients in heavyweight aluminum foil to saturate meat with liquids. Place in Dutch Oven and bake at 225° F for eight hours. Last hour unfold foil and turn up heat to 375°F.

Discard juice and slice meat. Top with favorite barbecue or horseradish sauce.

FOR SANDWICHES: Shred the cooked meat and add the can of chicken broth. Serve on kaiser rolls with barbecue, horseradish or mustard sauce.

Per serving: 311 Calories; 14g Fat (43% calories from fat); 40g Protein; 1g Carbohydrate; 94mg Cholesterol; 751mg Sodium

Suggested Wine: *Gamay Beaujolais or dry Rosé*

Chili

For chili lovers only and not for the faint of heart.

Serving Size: 14

3 medium onions, diced
1 medium green pepper, diced
1 medium sweet red pepper, diced
2 medium mild yellow pepper, diced
2 stalks celery, diced
6 cloves garlic, finely chopped
2 jalapeño chili peppers, diced
2 tablespoons olive oil
3 pounds lean ground beef
3 pounds sirloin steaks, trimmed and cubed
4 ounces dry red wine
29 ounces diced tomatoes with green chilies
6 ounces tomato paste
15 ounces tomato sauce
6 tablespoons chili powder
3 tablespoons cumin powder
6 whole bay leaves
6 ounces beer
freshly ground salt and pepper to taste
Tabasco sauce or other hot sauce to taste
mineral water

Place meat in bowl with wine, cover and let marinate for 1 to 2 hours in fridge.

Dice and sauté first seven ingredients in oil. Add meat (with wine) and remaining ingredients, including 1/2 can of beer (drink the rest). Add water just to cover top. Cook about 3 hours on low heat. Stir often. Freezes well.

Per serving: 498 Calories; 28g Fat (52% calories from fat); 41g Protein; 18g Carbohydrate; 132mg Cholesterol; 457mg Sodium

Suggested Wine: *Zinfandel*

Q: Do you have any recipes using wine with shellfish?

A: Here are several:

Shrimp a la Mikrolimano

This recipe was given to me by a chef on a cruise line as we visited the beautiful Greek Islands.

Serving Size: 6

30 medium raw shrimp, peeled and deveined
6 ounces Feta cheese, crumbled
4 ounces grated Parmesan cheese
16 ounces canned whole tomato, without juice
1 medium carrot, chopped
1 small onion, chopped
1 small green pepper, seeded and chopped
4 stalks celery with leaves
1 teaspoon oregano
1/3 cup dry white wine
1 tablespoon butter
salt and pepper to taste

Freshly chop carrot, onion, green pepper and celery. Sauté in a medium-sized saucepan in half the butter until the onion is golden. Remove the vegetables and in the same pan, add remaining butter. When bubbling, add the whole shrimp, stirring for 2-3 minutes. Add the wine, cook on medium heat for another 2-3 minutes, then return the vegetables to the pan, along with the chopped tomatoes and pepper and salt to taste. Scoop 5 shrimp with vegetables into individual ramekins or put entire contents of saucepan into an ovenproof dish. Sprinkle with crumbled Feta, then with the grated Parmesan. Place dish or ramekins into a very hot oven, 425-450°F, for 5 minutes until the cheeses melt. Serve at once by itself or on a bed of rice.

Per serving: 291 Calories; 15g Fat (48% calories from fat); 26g Protein; 11g Carbohydrate; 144mg Cholesterol; 816mg Sodium

Suggested Wine: *Sauvignon Blanc, Retsina or Chablis*

Risotto di Scampi

A simple yet delicious dish that is sure to please and impress.

Serving Size: 8

2 dozen raw jumbo shrimp, peeled and deveined
1 pound bay scallops
2 cups arborio rice
3 tablespoons extra virgin olive oil
4 cups fish or chicken stock
2 tablespoons butter
3 cloves minced garlic
1 cup dry white wine
salt and pepper to taste
2 tablespoons fresh parsley, chopped
1/3 cup Parmesan cheese

In a heated pot bring the olive oil and 1/2 cup of wine to a boil. Gently stir in the rice, covering each grain of rice with the oil mixture, allowing the rice grains to be heated thoroughly.

Add 4 cups of boiling broth to the rice. Stir, cover and let simmer on low heat for 18 minutes.

In a sauté pan melt butter, add garlic and rest of wine. Add shrimp (cut into chunks), scallops, salt and pepper and cook until slightly firm. When risotto is done, gently stir in the seafood mix with the juice, cheese and chopped parsley.

Simmer for additional 2-3 minutes and serve immediately.

Per serving: 383 Calories; 12g Fat (33% calories from fat); 16g Protein; 41g Carbohydrate;472mg Cholesterol; 324mg Sodium

Suggested Wine: *Pinot Grigio, Soave or Chablis*

Shrimp Butter

Serving Size: 4

1 tablespoon Italian seasoning mixture
1/2 teaspoon crushed red pepper flakes
2 tablespoons butter
1 teaspoon lemon juice
1/8 cup dry white wine

Melt butter and mix in all ingredients. Baste on shrimp as they cook on the grill.

Per serving 56 Calories; 6g Fat (98% calories from fat); 0g Protein; 0g Carbohydrate; 15mg Cholesterol; 58mg Sodium

NOTES

_____

_____

_____

_____

_____

_____

_____

_____

Q: Do you have any recipe suggestions for spaghetti sauce using wine?

A: Is my name Italian? Here are two of my personal recipes starting with a variation of Marcella Hazan's classic recipe.

Joe's "Bolognese Ragu"

Serving Size: 8

2 cloves minced garlic
2 tablespoons olive oil
2 tablespoons butter
1 medium white onion, finely chopped
2/3 cup chopped celery
2/3 cup chopped carrots
1/4 pound pancetta or bacon, diced
1/2 pound ground chuck
1/2 pound bulk Italian sausage, out of skins
1 cup milk
1/2 teaspoon fresh, grated or ground nutmeg
1/4 teaspoon ground cloves
1 cup dry red wine (Italian, of course)
1 1/2 cups diced or crushed canned tomatoes
1 tablespoon fresh basil, finely chopped
salt and pepper to taste

Sauté the pancetta, garlic and onion in the olive oil and butter over medium high heat until the onions have become translucent (do not burn). Then add the chopped celery and carrot. Cook for about 2 minutes, stirring the vegetables to coat them well

Add the ground meat with a pinch of salt and a little fresh ground pepper. Crumble the meat while mixing in the vegetables, stirring until the meat has lost its raw, red color.

Add the milk and let it simmer, gently stirring frequently until the milk is nearly gone. Add the nutmeg and ground cloves, stir. Add the wine and let it simmer until it has evaporated, then add the tomatoes and basil, stir thoroughly to coat all ingredients well. When the tomatoes begin to bubble, turn the heat down so that the sauce cooks at the lowest simmer.

Cook, uncovered, for an hour or more, stirring from time to time. Add 1/2 cup of water to keep it from drying out too quickly and sticking to the pan. In the end, however, no water at all must be left.

Toss with 1 1/2 pounds of your favorite pasta, but *tagliatelle* is the classic Bolognese pasta used for this sauce. *Rigatoni, fusilli* or noodles for baked lasagne are also delicious with this sauce.

Per serving: 317 Calories; 23g Fat (71% calories from fat); 15g Protein; 7g Carbohydrate; 65mg Cholesterol; 766mg Sodium

Suggested Wine: *Serve with a Chianti Classico Riserva or Armarone.*

NOTES

_____

_____

_____

_____

_____

_____

_____

_____

_____

"Old World" Spaghetti Sauce

The family recipe!

Serving Size: 8

2 pounds pork loin or Italian sausage links
2 tablespoons olive oil
6 ounces tomato paste
30 ounces crushed canned tomatoes in purée
1 cup red wine
2 cups water
2 bay leaf leaves
2 tablespoons chopped basil leaves, fresh preferred
1 tablespoon oregano, dried or fresh
1 tablespoon fresh parsley
4 large onions, finely chopped
4 ounces roasted red peppers, puréed or finely chopped
salt and pepper to taste

Brown pork roast or Italian sausage links in olive oil in 6-8 quart heavy pot. Remove meat, cover and set aside. Sauté finely chopped onion and garlic in the meat fat and olive oil until translucent. Add rest of ingredients. Blend well and bring to hard boil over medium-high heat, then down to lowest heat to simmer for about 4 to 5 hours. Cool or refrigerate overnight.

Skim excess grease next day and simmer another 2-3 hours. Add water or wine if too thick. Boil with cover off if too thin.

Note: The longer and slower the simmer - the better!

Per serving: 239 Calories; 10g Fat (38% calories from fat); 22g Protein; 13g Carbohydrate; 47mg Cholesterol; 408mg Sodium

Q: How about some pasta recipes using wine?

A: As quickly as you can say, *Mangia Bene!* (Eat Well). Here are a few of my favorites.

Fettuccine Quattro Fromaggi

Serving Size: 8

1 pound fettucine, cooked
1/2 cup dry white wine
1 tablespoon butter
1/2 cup Havarti cheese, grated
1/2 cup Farmer's cheese, grated
1/2 cup Gorgonzola cheese, crumbled
1/2 cup Parmesan cheese, grated
1/2 cup half and half
fresh ground black pepper to taste

Heat the slightly under-cooked fettucine noodles in the butter and white wine.

Add the Havarti, Farmer's, Gorgonzola and Parmesan cheese and stir only until melted and blended under medium-high heat.

Pour in the cream and add ground black pepper, continue stirring until thick.

Serve immediately.

Note: As the main entrée, this recipe can be embellished with spinach fettuccine and any combination of pine nuts, fresh mushrooms, peas, grilled chicken breast or veal strips, chopped ham or shrimp. This recipe also works well as a rich risotto dish.

Per serving: 348 Calories; 12g Fat (32% calories from fat); 15g Protein; 44g Carbohydrate; 30mg Cholesterol; 299mg Sodium

Suggested Wine: Pinot Grigio or Sauvignon Blanc

Thunder and Lightning

This recipe comes from my friend Brian Cain, who happens to be one of the most knowledgeable wine retailers I know.

Serving Size: 4

8 ounces medium-cut shell pasta
1/4 cup extra virgin olive oil
3 cloves garlic, peeled & minced
2 cups canned garbanzo beans (chick peas), drained
1 teaspoon dried sage
1 cup chicken stock
1/2 cup dry white wine
1 1/2 teaspoons cracked black pepper (red pepper flakes, optional)
2 tablespoons butter
1/2 cup grated Parmesan cheese

Cook pasta "al dente," drain and blend in butter.

In a 12" skillet, heat oil, add garlic and garbanzo beans and cook over high heat until the beans start to pop, hence, "Thunder & Lightning."

Add sage, stock, wine and pepper. Lower heat and cook until liquid is reduced by half and starts to thicken (at this point you may add spinach leaves, fresh mushrooms, sorrel, cubed grilled chicken breasts, garden peas, escarole or arugula, if desired).

Add the garbanzos, broth mixture and a 1/4 cup of the grated cheese to the pasta. Toss well and serve immediately in warm bowls with Italian bread and the remaining cheese.

Note: A delicious dish made and served with Sauvignon Blanc.

Per serving: 830 Calories; 30g Fat (33% calories from fat); 32g Protein; 105g Carbohydrate; 25mg Cholesterol; 860mg Sodium

Risotto al Limone

If you like pasta then you'll also like this easy risotto recipe that my wife, Barbara, perfected.

Serving Size: 8

4 cups low sodium chicken broth
1/2 cup dry white wine
2 cups Italian arborio rice
1 stick butter
2 tablespoons olive oil
1/2 cup Parmesan cheese, freshly grated
1 egg yolk
juice of 1 lemon
rind of 1 lemon, finely grated

Add broth and wine to a saucepan. Bring to a boil and keep it simmering.

Melt half the butter ("I Can't Believe It's Not Butter" is a good butter substitute) in sauté pan or 4 quart saucepan. Add oil. Stir in rice until it is totally coated. Add all of the boiling broth and stir thoroughly. Cover pan and reduce heat to a low simmer for twenty minutes. Do not disturb the cover during this time.

Beat the egg yolk with the lemon juice, then add the grated rind. When grating the rind, do not include the white part, which is very bitter. At the end of the twenty minutes, remove the rice from the heat for a moment so the yolk won't cook as you add it to the rice. Add yolk along with the Parmesan and the rest of the butter.

Place back on heat and stir for a minute or so. Taste the rice — it should be "al dente" or slightly firm to the tooth. Plate and serve immediately.

If desired, you may offer more grated cheese at the table.

Refrigerate any leftovers. May be baked or made into patties and sautéed in butter as a starch side-dish.

Note: This dish is particularly suited for a summer luncheon or a light dinner. A chilled bottle of Pinot Grigio or Pinot Gris makes a wonderful wine companion for this tasty recipe served with grilled chicken or veal chops.

Per serving: 258 Calories; 7g Fat (24% calories from fat); 11g Protein; 38g Carbohydrate; 34mg Cholesterol; 377mg Sodium

Q: Does cooking with white wine improve chicken recipes?

A: I think so, but try these and decide for yourself.

Chicken Marinade

Serving Size: 4

12 ounces low-fat Caesar's dressing (Ken's or Kraft)
1 teaspoon anchovy paste
1/2 cup dry white wine

Mix together and pour over skinless chicken breasts. Place covered in refrigerator for 3-4 hours. Great on the grill.

Chicken Spiedini with Prosciutto and Gorgonzola

One of my personal favorites. A delicious, full-flavored entrée when accompanied by a cheese and cream risotto or pasta.

Serving Size: 4

4 skinless, boneless chicken breast halves
4 ounces prosciutto, thinly sliced
4 ounces sun-dried tomatoes
2/3 cup crumbled Gorgonzola cheese
1/2 teaspoon ground sage
1/4 cup walnuts, finely chopped
2 tablespoons extra virgin olive oil
1 cup dry white wine
salt and pepper to taste

Soften the sun-dried tomatoes by soaking them in warm water for 1/2 to 1 hour.

Place each chicken breast between two pieces of plastic wrap. Using a food mallet, pound until about 1/4 inch thick. Remove the plastic wrap and place the flattened pieces on a clean work surface.

Top each chicken breast with 1 ounce of prosciutto, one sun-dried tomato (place widthwise), one fourth of the crumbled Gorgonzola (Italian blue cheese), 1/8 teaspoon of sage and a fourth of the chopped walnuts.

Roll up the chicken breasts with the toppings and wrap tightly in plastic wrap. Refrigerate the newly-created spiedini rolls for at least 1 hour. When ready to prepare, remove the plastic wrap from the chicken spiedini and secure with toothpicks. Sprinkle with salt and pepper. In a large skillet heat oil until hot. Add spiedini and brown on all sides. Turn frequently. Add wine and simmer covered for 10 to 15 minutes, depending on the thickness of the spiedini rolls.

Remove spiedini rolls to a clean cutting board and cover with foil to keep warm.

Reduce wine to half over medium-high heat. Strain into a glass bowl.

Slice each chicken spiedini vertically into 1/4 to 1/2 inch slices. Place slices, slightly overlapping each other, on individual dishes. Drizzle with wine sauce and serve.

Per serving: 395 Calories; 18g Fat (41% calories from fat); 42g Protein; 17g Carbohydrate; 99mg Cholesterol; 1695mg Sodium

Suggested Wine: *Australian Chardonnay or any dry, white Italian wine*

NOTES

_____

_____

_____

_____

_____

Chicken Bianco

Serving Size: 6

1/3 cup olive oil
1/4 cup butter
1 1/2 pounds skinless, boneless chicken breasts
1 cup flour
salt and fresh ground black pepper to taste
1 1/2 cups dry white wine
2 tablespoons lemon zest
5 tablespoons fresh parsley, finely chopped

Pound chicken breasts slightly so the thickness is nearly the same on each. Put the oil and butter in a large sauté or fry pan and heat on medium-high. Dredge the chicken breasts in the flour, on both sides. When the butter foam begins to subside, place the breasts in the pan without overlapping. Brown the meat well on both sides. Season liberally with salt and freshly ground pepper. Add the white wine and cover the pan tightly. Turn the heat down so the juices in the pan bubble gently on low simmer. The meat must cook very slowly, until it becomes tender, about 25 minutes.

After 10 or 15 minutes, when there is very little liquid in the pan, add 1/2 cup warm water. Check the pan from time to time, and add more warm water as needed. The meat is done when it is tender enough to be cut with a fork. When done, transfer the chicken to a warm platter.

Add the lemon peel and chopped parsley to the pan and heat to medium. Cook for about a minute, stirring with a wooden spoon and scraping loose any cooking bits stuck to the pan. Boil down any excess liquid. Return the chicken to the pan and very briefly turn them in the pan juices. Serve at once with all the pan juices poured over the chicken.

Per serving: 421 Calories; 22g Fat (52% calories from fat); 29g Protein; 17g Carbohydrate; 86mg Cholesterol; 160mg Sodium

Suggested Wine: *Fume Blanc or Soave*

Grilled Chicken with Olives

The distinctive tangy taste of this dish takes chicken to a new level.

Serving Size: 6

1 cup minced green olives
1 medium diced red bell pepper
6 skinless boneless chicken breast halves
juice of 2 lemons
1/4 cup extra virgin olive oil
sea salt to taste
1/4 cup dry white wine
1 teaspoon Italian parsley, minced

Mix the olives and red pepper in a bowl; spread over the chicken, add the juice of one lemon and refrigerate for two hours.

Drain the chicken (reserving the solids from the marinade), brush with the olive oil, season with salt and cook on a medium-hot grill for 12 to 15 minutes or in a preheated broiler for 10 minutes.

Cook the solids from the marinade in the remaining olive oil until aromatic, about 3 minutes. Deglaze with the wine and remaining lemon juice, cook 2 minutes. Add salt and parsley.

Pour over the chicken and serve hot with broiled new potatoes or a cream, cheese or mushroom sauce over your favorite pasta or risotto.

Per serving: 215 Calories; 13g Fat (57% calories from fat); 21g Protein; 1g Carbohydrate; 51mg Cholesterol; 645mg Sodium

Suggested Wine: *Sauvignon Blanc or dry Riesling*

Chicken Rice Salad

At a picnic or the dining table — a refreshingly different salad course.

Serving Size: 10

1 pound skinless boneless chicken breasts
1 1/2 cups Arborio rice
2 1/2 cups fat-free chicken broth (Swanson's low salt)
2/3 cup dry white wine
3 tablespoons olive oil
1 bunch white seedless grapes
1/2 cup toasted slivered almonds
8 ounces crumbled Feta cheese
3/4 teaspoon celery seed

Marinate chicken breasts in a bottled caesar salad dressing overnight.

One hour before preparing recipe, grill the chicken over medium heat until pink just disappears in meat. Do not over cook. Set aside in glass bowl and cover. Discard marinade.

Bring chicken stock and wine to a boil in a separate sauce pan (add any juice from the standing grilled chicken).

Sauté rice in olive oil in 6 to 8 quart pot constantly stirring until all the rice grains are coated with oil, about 2 to 3 minutes. Stir in the boiling liquid mixture until thoroughly blended. Put on cover and turn heat to low. Simmer for 20 minutes without removing the cover.

While simmering, prepare remaining ingredients. Cut grilled chicken into cubes and seedless grapes in half. Toast slivered almonds. Crumble Feta cheese. Mix all ingredients, except Feta, in the chicken bowl (don't lose any of the juices). Add celery seed.

At exactly 20 minutes from starting the simmer, take off cover and add the ingredient mixture. Blend thoroughly. Replace cover and allow to simmer for 3 to 5 minutes or until rice has a firm, but not hard feel to the tooth — "al dente."

Refrigerate for at least one hour before serving. Add the crumbled Feta after the risotto cools. Can be made the day before. Serve slightly chilled with a medium body, dry white wine, Sauvignon Blanc, Riesling or Pinot Grigio. Garnish with fresh parsley.

Per serving: 305 Calories; 13g Fat (38% calories from fat); 20g Protein; 27g Carbohydrate; 47mg Cholesterol; 420mg Sodium

Marinated Roasted Peppers

Great garnish for chicken or steak. Excellent on pizza or bruschetta, too.

Serving Size: 6

2 tablespoons extra virgin olive oil
1 large red bell pepper, halved and cleaned
1 large yellow bell pepper, halved and cleaned
1 large green bell pepper, halved and cleaned
1 large onion, halved lengthwise
4 cloves garlic, finely chopped
1/8 cup white wine vinegar
2 tablespoons balsamic vinegar
1 teaspoon sea salt
fresh ground white pepper to taste
1/2 teaspoon red pepper flakes (optional)
2 Roma tomatoes, chopped
2 tablespoons fresh basil, finely chopped

Roast the peppers, whole garlic cloves and onion halves on the grill (or broiler) until slightly charred. Do not overdo veggies. Remove garlic cloves and chop and slice the peppers and onions into 1/2 inch strips. Transfer to glass bowl. Add the vinegars, olive oil, red pepper flakes and season with salt and pepper.

Cover and refrigerate until well-chilled. Overnight is best. Turn occasionally.

Add basil and tomatoes to pepper marinade and season again with salt and pepper before serving or topping pizza, bruschetta or focaccia.

Serve cold or at room temperature.

Note: Vidalia or red onions work best. Green pepper will add a little more bitterness to the mixture. Substitute with an orange sweet pepper if desired.

Per serving: 74 Calories; 5g Fat (54% calories from fat); 1g Protein; 8g Carbohydrate; 0mg Cholesterol; 319mg Sodium

Q: How about dessert recipes using wine and liqueurs?

A: Try one of these.

Chocolate Kahlua Cake

Sinfully delicious!

Serving Size: 16

CAKE
1 box plain devil's food cake mix
2 boxes instant chocolate pudding mix - small boxes
3/4 cup Kahlua
1/2 cup water
1/2 cup canola oil
4 large eggs

GANACHE
3/4 cup whipping cream
8 ounces semisweet chocolate, finely chopped
1 tablespoon Kahlua

CAKE: Place a rack in the center of the oven and preheat the oven to 350°F. Lightly mist a 12 cup bundt pan with vegetable oil spray, then dust with flour. Shake out the excess flour. Set the pan aside.

Place the cake mix, pudding mix, Kahlua, water, oil and eggs in a large mixing bowl. Blend with an electric mixer on low speed for 1 minute. Stop the machine and scrape down the sides of the bowl with a rubber spatula. Increase the mixer speed to medium and beat for 2 to 3 minutes more, scraping the sides down again if needed. The batter should look thick and smooth. Pour the batter into the prepared pan, smoothing it out with the rubber spatula. Place the pan in the oven.

Bake the cake until it springs back when lightly pressed with your finger and a toothpick inserted into the center comes out clean, 45 to 50 minutes. Remove the pan from the oven and place it on a wire rack to cool for 20 minutes. Run a long, sharp knife around the edge of the cake and invert it on a serving platter. Let cool.

GANACHE: Place the cream in a small heavy saucepan over medium heat. Bring to a boil, stirring. Meanwhile, place the chopped chocolate in a large mixing bowl. Remove the pan from the heat and pour the hot cream over the chopped chocolate. Stir until the chocolate is melted. Stir in the Kahlua.

To use the ganache as a glaze, let it stand at room temperature for 10 minutes before spooning over a cooled cake. To use the ganache as a frosting, let it stand at room temperature for 4 hours, or chill it until it thickens and is spreadable.

Per serving: 372 Calories; 19g Fat (47% calories from fat); 3g Protein; 45g Carbohydrate; 61mg Cholesterol; 354mg Sodium

NOTES

_____

_____

_____

_____

_____

_____

_____

_____

_____

Rice Fritters in Strawberry Sauce

Like eating "angel fritters from heaven."

Serving Size: 6

SAUCE
1/4 cup raspberries
1/4 cup blueberries
1/4 cup blackberries
1/4 cup lemon juice or juice of 1 lemon
2 cups strawberries, hulled & diced
2 1/2 tablespoons sugar
1 cup dry red wine

FRITTERS
2 cups whole milk
1 1/4 cups sugar
1/2 cup rice, Balilla variety
1/4 cup all-purpose flour, unbleached
2 large eggs, separated
1 large pear, peeled, cored and diced
peanut oil (about 3 cups for frying)
1 cup semolina flour (available at specialty grocery stores)

SAUCE: Blend the raspberries, blackberries and blueberries with the lemon juice in a food processor until smooth. Toss with the strawberries, sugar and wine in a bowl. Refrigerate for a least 4 hours.

FRITTERS: Bring the milk and 1/4 cup of sugar to a boil in a 1 quart pot. Add the rice; cook, stirring often to prevent sticking, until the milk has been absorbed and rice is creamy and cooked, about 30 minutes over medium-low heat. Spoon onto a tray and cool to room temperature. Fold in the flour, egg yolks and pear. In a clean bowl, beat the egg whites until soft peaks form. Fold into the rice mixture.

Heat the oil in a shallow pan until it registers 375°F. Roll spoonfuls of the rice mixture in the semolina flour; drop a few at a time in the hot oil. Fry, turning to cook evenly, until golden on all sides, about 3 minutes. Remove with a slotted spoon to a platter lined with paper towels. Blot dry. Dredge the fritters in the remaining sugar and serve hot, with the sauce.

Note: Rolling the rice mixture in semolina flour make the fritters crunchy. Use all-purpose flour for a softer consistency.

Per serving: 503 Calories; 5g Fat (9% calories from fat); 10g Protein; 100g Carbohydrate; 72mg Cholesterol; 85mg Sodium

Suggested Wine: *Asti Spumante*

NOTES

_____

_____

_____

_____

_____

_____

_____

_____

_____

Fruit Whoopee!

This refreshing wine and fruit combination utilizes the fresh fruit of the season or whatever is currently being shipped in to your local grocery store. It is much better to use fresh fruit as opposed to frozen or canned.

Serving Size: 8

1/2 fresh watermelon
1/2 pint fresh raspberries
1/2 pint fresh blueberries
1/2 pint fresh strawberries
1/2 pint fresh cherries
1/2 fresh cantaloupe, cubed
1 750ml bottle of May Wine, Semi-Dry Riesling or
    Gewürztraminer wine, chilled

Hollow out the half watermelon by making watermelon balls (avoiding the seeds as much as possible) and placing the balls in a bowl. Peel and cube the half cantaloupe after cleaning out the seeds. Wash, hull and pit all other fruit and mix with the watermelon and cantaloupe.

Return the fruit mixture to the hollowed-out watermelon shell and pour in the wine. Cover with plastic wrap and let marinate in the refrigerator for an hour or so. Serve chilled in your largest wine glasses for an elegant dessert or afternoon treat.

Use the watermelon shell for a table centerpiece...and second helpings.

Per serving: 116 Calories; 1g Fat (10% calories from fat); 2g Protein; 27g Carbohydrate; 0mg Cholesterol; 8mg Sodium

Serving and Dining with Wine

For wine to taste like wine, it should be drunk with a friend.

SPANISH PROVERB

•

A true friend always brings a bottle of wine to dinner.

JOE BORRELLO

Q: Should wine always be served at room temperature?

A: Room temperature for wine is around 65°F: and that is a rather cool room for a house. The term room temperature dates back to before central heating. Fifteen minutes in the refrigerator should bring a red wine to your desired temperature. Chilling much more than 65°F, however, does retard the flavor of most red wines.

Q: I see advertisements that say this restaurant or that one has an excellent wine list. In a restaurant what constitutes a good wine list?

A: In my opinion, a good wine list is not necessarily the most extensive one, but rather one that has been carefully created to offer an adequate selection of wine to complement the menu entrées. A good wine list should always take into consideration the chef's entrée preparations.

Q: Does sediment in the bottle mean the wine has gone bad?

A: The sediment is a completely natural part of the aging process for some wines. By decanting the wine into another container, you can separate the sediment before drinking the wine. Place the bottle upright for a couple of hours so the sediment settles before pouring. Be sure to pour slowly, so you don't disturb the sediment. It will not harm you, but it does have a slightly bitter taste. Decanting the wine is an age-old tradition that can benefit the wine by enhancing both the clarity and flavor.

Q: Is it necessary to open a bottle of wine and let it be exposed to the air before serving?

A: Younger wines have a tendency to need aeration in order to release and develop their aromas, soften tannins and awaken the flavors. With older wines, however, you may be taking a chance in overexposing them to oxygen. The best bet is to open all wines when you are ready to serve them. If the wine needs airing, it will develop quickly in the glass. As it improves, everyone will have the pleasure of following its progress. At the same time, you have eliminated any risk of overexposing a wine that did not need to breathe beforehand.

Q: How do I go about putting together a wine tasting party for friends?

A: Sampling some of nature's most fascinating nectar is a rewarding and deceptively simple pleasure. A planned wine tasting requires that you use your senses of sight, smell and taste. It offers the opportunity to explore the subtleties of wine and to refine your ability to enjoy wine — all at a controlled cost, with friends who share your interest.

The first thing you have to determine is the theme. For instance, "The Great Wines of Bordeaux," "Sparkling Wines of the World" or "The Foods and Wines of the Northwest." The possibilities are endless, and your local wine merchant will be of invaluable help in the planning. After you have determined a wine and food menu (dinner or appetizers) think about the service. Glasses should be stemware so the warmth of the hand will not alter the temperature of the wine as your party progresses. Inexpensive, clear stemware found in almost any department store is quite sufficient. For sparkling wines, never use the wide-rimmed Champagne glass. The fascination of these wines lies mainly in their bubbles. Unfortunately, the wide-rimmed glasses allow the natural gases to vanish much too quickly, and half the enchantment is lost.

To experience the full pleasure of wine, serve it at the correct temperature and bring it to that temperature slowly and gently. Red wines are served at room temperature (around 60 to 65°F). Dry white wines and rosé wines are served chilled, but not overly so. Sweet white wines and sparkling wines are served colder. No wine, however, should be too cold, or its flavor will be muted.

When you serve the wine, fill glasses only one-third to one-half full, so you will not have to worry about anyone swirling wine on to your Belgian lace tablecloth. Expect to serve about six glasses from each 750ml bottle unless you are serving more than four wines, in which case, each bottle can be stretched to serve eight to ten guests.

Wine is appreciated by color, aroma and taste. The two aspects of color are clarity and hue. A sound wine is bright and clear; its hue tells us its type, age and substance. As wine ages, its color changes. Red wines generally lose their vibrant shades and become lighter, changing to a brick color in old age. White wines become darker, changing finally to old gold.

Swirl the glass gently to aerate the wine and release its bouquet. Inhale the aroma..ahh! Our first and most important impression of a wine comes from the smell. Smell helps us define how fruity or flowery a wine is and to point out both positive and negative qualities.

After you have evaluated color and bouquet, you should have a good idea of how the wine will taste. Now you are ready to sample it. Take a sip and swirl it around in your mouth to get the full flavor, to distinguish sweet, sour, bitter and salty tastes, and to judge the weight of the wine, i.e. whether it's full or light-bodied.

Sweetness is readily apparent in any wine that has residual sugar. Bitterness usually indicates the presence of tannin, which comes from grape skins and is an important natural ingredient for the long-lasting quality of fine red wines. The tannin in young wine gives it an astringent, puckerish trait. As wine matures, the tannin decreases and the wine develops a smoother, rounder taste. Acidity is a key component of all wine, especially white wine. A wine with too much acidity tastes tart and unpleasant; one with too little acidity tastes "flabby." One with balanced acidity tastes fresh and lively.

There, you have it. With a little care and preparation, you and your guests can experience the joys of wine. Herein lies the key to a successful wine tasting — ENJOY! That is what it's all about, pure and simple.

Q: At a wine tasting party, in what order should red, blush, white and sparkling wines be served?

A: As a general rule, serve white wines before reds and dry wines before sweet. Blush wines are served as you would rosé, in-between the white and the red wines. The serving order is a matter of commonsense, rather than one of etiquette. Sweet wines have a tendency to overpower the taste buds, which will give the sensation of bitterness to dry wines after the palate has been stimulated with sweetness. Heartier red wines have the same effect over white wines, so it only makes sense to serve in the suggested order to get the most enjoyment from the wines. Sparkling wines, with their higher acid content and bubbles, have a tendency to clear and cleanse the palate, so they may be served first or last with no loss in taste.

Q: My wine merchant said I should only use clear stemware for wine glasses. Why is that?

A: Wine appreciation is a combination of our senses of sight, smell and taste. Since sight offers our first impression of the wine, and our eyes prepare our taste buds for the pleasures that will follow, your wine merchant correctly suggested clear glass to show the beauty of the wine. Decorations only detract from the real pleasure within the glass. Stemware is also preferable, so body heat does not affect the temperature of the wine. Most importantly, the bowl of the glass should be large enough for the wine to be swirled freely and release the full aroma without fear of spilling. An eight to twelve-ounce glass works perfectly, as long as it is not filled more than half way full. It is not necessary to have a different style of glass for various wine types. But it is recommended that a fresh glass be used for the presentation of each new wine. This will prevent the mixing of subtle flavors. If this is not possible, provide bottled water to rinse the glasses after tasting each wine.

Q: In a restaurant recently, I refilled a glass of wine for my date and received a glaring stare from our waiter. Did I commit a major social blunder?

A: Not in my book, you didn't! It is your money, and you should be allowed to pour your own wine, especially if your service person is not paying attention to the service at your table. If, however, it is your intention to do the pouring throughout the meal, you might mention your intention to the service person to avoid those icy stares.

Q: The wine I ordered at a restaurant was brought already opened to the table. The service person poured a little for me to taste, but for some reason I felt I was being served a bottle somebody else rejected. Was I being paranoid?

A: Maybe a little. Once you have ordered a bottle of wine it should always be presented at the table to verify your selection before it is opened. But it was more likely a case of an inexperienced server who needed help from the bartender than a "fast one" being pulled by the restaurant. Then again, wine-server training is not the customer's problem. The bottle should have been presented, then taken to the bar to be opened. I would advise against accepting a bottle of wine that has been opened before it reaches the table, paranoid or not.

Q: As a restaurant waiter, what is the correct way for me to serve wine?

A: First, the wine list should be presented at the same time as the menu. More and more, people are ordering wine before dinner instead of cocktails. After the wine is ordered, always present the bottle, unopened, to the table for verification. Cut the foil about a half inch down from the bottle lip and wipe off the top. After pulling the cork, place it on the table for anyone who wants to examine it. An ounce or so of wine is poured in the glass of the person who ordered the wine for approval of clarity, aroma, temperature and finally, taste. All should meet with satisfaction. Wine glasses should be spotless and large enough to be filled only halfway to allow room for the wine's bouquet to develop. The customer is paying for the wine and is entitled to enjoy it to the fullest.

Q: What type of wine can I give as a gift that does not have to be stored for years before it can be enjoyed?

A: Many people are of the misconception that the longer they keep a wine, the better or more valuable it will become. Contrary to this popular belief, most of the world's wine is consumed within a few years of bottling. As a matter of fact, if the majority of the world's wine was aged for a long period of time, it would more than likely deteriorate in quality. Almost any wine found on the retail shelves would be appropriate as a gift to be consumed within the next year or two. If you are the recipient of such a gift, enjoy the wine while it is fresh, fruity and full of life. The super premium wines would be the only exception and your local wine merchant is your best guide to those products.

Q: What is May Wine?

A: May Wine, a creation of German winemakers, is a semi-sweet, light, white wine flavored with the aromatic herb, woodruff. It is traditionally produced and released in the spring of the year. May Wine is delicious when well chilled and poured over fresh strawberries or other fresh fruit of the season. Simple and elegant, served in a wine glass, this combination sets an impressive table and is a refreshing dessert. In the United States, St. Julian Wine Company in Michigan and The Brotherhood Winery in New York make a May Wine.

Q: Are fruit wines better by themselves than at the dinner table?

A: Fruit wines make refreshing cocktails, punches and *aperitifs* when mixed with sparkling soda, white wine or served over ice. As far as an accompaniment with food, fruit wines are an excellent addition to many food recipes. They enrich sauces and desserts, and nothing is more tasty than a turkey, chicken or ham that is basted with a peach, cherry or raspberry wine. When using fruit wines for basting or sauces, serve a medium-dry white or sparkling wine with the dish. For desserts, try fruit wines over a bowl of fresh fruit or in your special mousse recipe. There are dozens of dessert recipes, from cakes to ice cream, that explode with flavor when fruit wines are added.

Q: Is there such a thing as a breakfast wine?

A: Ever try a little Champagne with your Rice Krispies? For a real snap, crackle and POP, nothing is more elegant and refreshing than sparkling wine with breakfast or brunch, particularly if you are entertaining. Just about any type or brand will do nicely. German-style, semi-dry white wines with subtle fruit flavors also complement breakfast entrées.

Q: Am I required to tip the wine steward in a restaurant?

A: You are not required to tip for restaurant service, unless it is the policy of the establishment to include it on the bill, but it certainly is expected. The usual gratuity for wine service is 10% to 15% of the wine bill, but no less than $2.00 per bottle, given directly to the wine steward. In some restaurants the wine service is performed by the management instead of a designated wine person. When this occurs, the evening's total check will include the wine and you should tip as you would normally. A separate tip is not necessary or expected, in this case.

Q: Why won't soap and water remove the cloudy film from the bottom of my wine decanter?

A: Wine left sitting in a decanter for an extended period of time will leave a cloudy film so that plain soap and water will not budge it. Fill the decanter with water and drop in an Alka-Seltzer tablet, allowing it to sit for a short time. Then wash it in warm soapy water and rinse with ammonia. Rinse again, thoroughly, with plain water. You can prevent the problem by not leaving wine or liqueurs in a decanter overnight and always rinsing it thoroughly right after use. Distilled products do not affect crystal the same way because they do not contain the same amount of acid as wine.

Q: What would be some good all-purpose wines to keep around the house for occasional guests?

A: If you do not know the wine tastes of your guests, you are usually safe with soft, light white wines that almost anyone would enjoy. Moderately priced wines such as a California French Colombard or Chenin Blanc, a regional Riesling or German Piesporter would be good choices. A soft Chilean Merlot, a California Blush wine or a Gamay Beaujolais will usually satisfy your red wine-drinking friends. Of course, any sparkling wine is a welcome refreshment for even the most discriminating guest. Just don't keep these light and easy wines around the house for too long or they will soon lose their charm.

Q: Could you suggest a few red wines that can be served slightly chilled without losing their character?

A: With arrival of warm weather, this question always presents a dilemma for red wine lovers. First, when we say serve red wine at room temperature you must remember this saying originated when drafty castles and chateaux were much cooler than 75 to 80°F. The saying should really be changed to "serve red wine at cellar temperature" which is closer to 65°F. If you are interested in a quality red wine that can be served at cooler temperatures, consider Gamay, Pinot Noir, Grenache and rosé or varietal blush wines from virtually anywhere in the world.

Q: What is the proper procedure for placing wine glasses on the dinner table?

A: It is preferable to have a fresh, clean glass for each wine planned with a meal. The glasses should be clear stemware and capable of holding eight to twelve ounces of wine. Etiquette dictates placing the wine glasses in the upper right hand portion of the place setting. The wines are poured one third to half full, from the first glass on the right of each guest (for the first course) to the last glass on the left (for dessert). If you do not have enough glasses for all the wines, use what you have and supply a pitcher of bottled water to rinse after each wine. There are some traditional wine glass shapes from various wine regions, but the all-purpose, 8 to 10 ounce tulip-shaped glass works very well for all types of wines.

Q: I received a hostess gift of wine from my dinner guests, but it did not match with the menu I had planned. Did I make a social blunder by not opening and serving the wine my friends brought?

A: The thoughtful gift was exactly that and is meant to be enjoyed by you at your leisure as a token of appreciation. If your friends expected to share the wine with you at dinner they should have told you ahead of time that they would like to bring the wine and asked for your recommendation to complement the menu.

Q: What is a vertical wine tasting?

A: A vertical wine tasting is a popular and fun theme for a wine tasting party with friends who share a common interest in learning about wine. A vertical tasting highlights a single variety of wine produced by one vintner, but spanning a number of different years. For example, you might like to select an interesting Merlot from any one winery. By comparing various vintages, say 1994 through 2000, you will have the opportunity to witness the development of this particular grape variety in both aging and in the winemaker's progress in establishing his individual style for handling the variety. It is sometimes difficult to obtain older vintages unless they have been collected in wine cellars or purchased directly from the winery. It may be easier, therefore, to host a horizontal wine tasting. In this tasting the Merlot, or any variety you choose, is presented from the same vintage from different wineries. With this tasting you get the opportunity to taste the difference in styles from winemakers using the same grape from the same harvest year.

Q: What is a waiter's corkscrew?

A: The waiter's corkscrew is the one that looks like a folded jackknife. Its spiral screw unfolds to a "T" with a leverage grip at one end and a cutting knife at the other. It is called a waiter's corkscrew because it is compact and easy for service people to carry around in their pocket. It does take some practice to become proficient with its use. The simplest and most inexpensive corkscrew to have around the kitchen is the popular wing corkscrew. The handles of this opener go up as the screw is turned into the cork. When the auger is all the way in, the handles are pushed down, forcing the cork up and out. However, do not use a corkscrew in opening a bottle of champagne. Use only your hands with the aid of a towel. Carefully twist the bottle with one hand while holding the cork with the other so the pressure inside will gradually force the cork out nice and easy.

Q: Is there any way to prevent a cork from breaking when opening a bottle of wine?

A: Most broken wine corks are due to inadequate corkscrews or poor technique in opening a bottle. First of all, you know you have the proper corkscrew when you can place a toothpick up the center of the worm. This type of auger will give a better grip in the cork, particularly if the cork is fragile. Secondly, be sure you screw the worm down the middle far enough to pierce the bottom of the cork and then pull out steadily. Twisting, jerking and bending a corkscrew in a cork will only increase your chances of loosing a firm hold and break the cork, or even worse, strip the core. With all your care, a cork may still break off in the bottle. At this point, try the corkscrew again or push the remaining solid cork into the bottle and carefully pour the wine over the cork and into a clear glass decanter which you may use to serve the wine.

Q: How much wine should I plan to serve for dinner guests?

A: That question is always a bit difficult to answer because there are variables. There are approximately six, four-ounce servings in a normal 750 ml wine bottle. At a quick luncheon, one serving per person might be enough, but at a long dinner party, three or four might not be too much. A total of half a bottle per person (combining different wines) is a reasonable average allowance for most people and occasions. But the circumstance and mood of the meal, and above all how long it goes on, are the deciding factors. There is a golden rule for hosts, "be generous, but never pressing."

Q: Do you have a recipe for Champagne Punch?

A: Here is a crowd pleaser for holiday parties.

Champagne Punch

50 ounces Champagne (2 bottles)
2 liters club soda
4 ounces Curacao or Triple Sec
4 ounces brandy
4 ounces maraschino cherry juice
1/2 cup of sugar

Mix together in a punch bowl with a large block of ice. Garnish with whole cherries, strawberries, orange or lemon slices.

If you are looking for something more grandiose, try the punch ordered by William III, who used a garden fountain as a giant punch bowl. The recipe included 560 gallons of brandy, 1,200 pounds of sugar, 25,000 lemons, 20 gallons of lime juice, and five pounds of nutmeg. The bartender rowed around in a small boat, filling up guests' punch cups.

For Personal Use

Wine moistens and tempers the spirits,
and lulls the care of the mind to rest…it
revives our joys.

SOCRATES

•

Give me a glass of an aged Barolo,
a fresh hunk of Parmigiano-Reggiano cheese,
a good football game on TV
and I'm contented.

JOE BORRELLO

Q: How can our family broaden our knowledge of wine?

A: Wine has been placed on dinner tables for centuries as a simple beverage that serves as a pleasing companion to food. Although many hours could be spent studying the finer points of wine makeup, don't complicate an enjoyable subject. True knowledge of wine comes only from personal tasting experiences. Through taste you acquire knowledge. You will find that not all wines are pleasing to you and that is how it should be. Wine, like food, is made in many different styles to satisfy different tastes. It is up to you to choose the wines that suit your palate and pocketbook. Seek guidance from others, but do not be intimidated by their opinions. Discover the wine treasures from around the world for yourself, starting with those made in your own backyard.

Q: How do I go about shopping for good wine values?

A: Wine is no different than anything else you shop for. Look for specials and featured wines that are not as well known as the more popular and expensive alternatives. This is also an excellent opportunity to taste different types of wines economically. Once you have found a few favorites, you will usually save 10 to 20% buying by the case. Most retail stores will give you a discount for mixed and multiple case purchases. Sometimes it is to your advantage to recruit a few friends and buy your wines together. It is a rather competitive industry and volume discounts, as well as individual bottle markdowns, are quite commonplace.

Q: How do I avoid becoming overwhelmed when trying to learn more about wine?

A: If you enjoy wine and food, you purchase wines regularly and desire to further your knowledge on the subject, then first observe your senses. Become aware of your likes and dislikes, just as you have done with food. Mentally record different tastes and aromas, particularly when combining wine with food. Soon you will be comparing various styles of wine and developing food and wine preferences. Begin reading articles in magazines and newspapers to fine tune your tastes. Lastly, meet with people who share your enthusiasm for food and wine, participate in group tastings and seminars. The best teacher of wine is experience. Continue to experiment and you will learn. You do not have to become a scholar of wine to enjoy its pleasures and benefits when consumed responsibly.

Q: How do I avoid purchasing a spoiled bottle of wine?

A: Shop at merchants who are experienced in selling wine and share your interest in tasting wine with food. Avoid wine stores that have bottles with labels discolored by age. That's a good sign that the inventory is old and not properly cared for. Bottles with corks should be stored horizontally to keep corks moist and airtight. Stores that are known to sell a large volume of wine will usually have a consistently fresh selection because of their frequent product turnover. Do not overlook inexpensive wines, they sometimes offer the best value in the store. Taste test freely with different styles and types of wine. When you find a wine you like, buy it in case lots, they are usually discounted. Always inspect the bottle's condition and, if by chance you purchase a wine that has gone bad, return it to the store.

Q: Is there an easy way to pick a wine from a restaurant's wine list?

A: A well-trained and knowledgeable service person is the most valuable asset to help with your selection. Rely on his or her knowledge of the restaurant's wine cellar, menu pairings and good values. Do not be afraid to ask questions. That is how you will learn.

Q: What is the best way to react when served a spoiled wine?

A: Cool, calm and collected - just like any other major crisis. Seriously, if it happens in a restaurant, simply inform the server and there should not be any problem with a replacement. Since wine is somewhat sensitive to outside elements, an occasional bad bottle does pop up through no fault of the restaurant or winery. If you receive a bad wine at a private residence, especially from home winemakers, that's a more delicate situation. The most diplomatic maneuver I have come across is from Robert Misch, the late New York wine writer who faced this predicament on numerous occasions. Misch would sip the wine, giving no facial clues revealing his dislike, ponder the taste, and with exuberance, announces, "Now, that's a wine!" Everyone was left to interpret what they wish.

Q: What is the best cure for the morning after an over-indulgence the night before?

A: The French call it "wood mouth," Germans refer to it as "wailing of the cats," Italians call it "out of tune," Norwegians identify it as "carpenters in the head," Spaniards call it "backlash," Swedes refer to it as "pain in the hair roots," and most English speaking countries call it "hangover." The ancient Greeks thought that eating cabbage would cure a hangover and the ancient Romans thought that eating fried canaries would do the same. Today, some Germans eat a breakfast of red meat and bananas, some French drink strong coffee with salt, some Chinese drink spinach tea, some Puerto Ricans rub half a lemon under their drinking arm, some Haitians stick thirteen black-headed needles into the cork of the bottle from which they drank, and some Russians drink vodka in an effort to cure hangovers. But by whatever name, it can always be prevented by drinking in moderation. None of the above cures are effective.

Q: What is the quickest way to chill a bottle of wine for dinner?

A: Place the bottle of wine in a bucket of half water and half ice. Within ten or fifteen minutes you will have a nicely chilled bottle of wine to be enjoyed by your dinner guests. Avoid adding ice cubes to the wine because as they melt they dilute the wine.

Q: What is the easiest procedure for opening a wine bottle?

A: There are four simple steps to opening a wine bottle:

1. Cut the foil cap covering the bottle opening about 1/4 inch below the lip of the bottle to ensure that the wine does not come in contact with the foil when poured. This is simply a sanitary precaution.
2. Wipe the mouth of the bottle with a clean cloth. Sometimes older wines have accumulated some "gunk." Do not be alarmed, just wipe it off.
3. Insert your corkscrew and extract the cork in one piece.
4. Wipe the mouth of the bottle again, including just inside the opening.

Now it is just a matter of pouring the wine for you and your guests to enjoy.

Q: Is there a trick to opening a bottle of Champagne?

A: No trick, just be careful. To open a bottle of Champagne or sparkling wine, first be sure the bottle is properly chilled. Now loosen the wine hood by untwisting the loop of wire which is just below the top of the cork and probably covered by a foil wrap. Having loosened the wire gently, without agitating the bottle, you will find the top of the foil capsule will come off easily. Then holding the bottle in your right hand, slightly incline at a 45° angle, and holding the cork in the left hand, twist the bottle. The inside pressure of the gas will help you to remove the cork fairly easily. Do not let it pop out or you may lose some wine and let a lot of the wine's gas escape before it can be enjoyed in the glass. Hold the cork tightly and let the gasses escape slowly. Now pour and enjoy, keeping the remaining wine in a cooler bucket.

Q: Does white wine really remove red wine stains?

A: Yes, white wine does seem to have a natural chemical reaction to eliminate red wine stains, as does applying club soda to the stain before it has set. If these do not work for you, try mixing salt and lemon juice and putting it on the stain. For laminate surfaces, make a paste of baking soda and lemon juice, spread over the stained area and let dry.

Q: I have four bottles of wine that include 1976 Lafite Rothchild and 1971 Mouton Rothchild. I was told the wines are worth about $1000. Would you recommend putting an ad in my local newspaper to sell them?

A: First of all, the $1000 figure seems a bit high to me, even for retail prices. Secondly, unless you are licensed by the Liquor Control Agency in your state, you are in violation of state laws if you try to sell the wine. Too often, people buy expensive bottles of wine as investments only to find out later that it is illegal to re-sell them in their state. Even in the states of Illinois and California, where it is possible to re-sell wines to collectors, single bottles are not sought after unless they are extremely rare and old. The best investment in wine is to consider your purchase as a hedge against inflation. As your wine becomes more scarce and in demand the retail price will go up and you will still be able to enjoy the wine at the lower original cost. To answer your question directly, no, I would not recommend putting an ad in your local newspaper to sell your collection. Save them and enjoy them with friends and family at some future special occasion. Both wines, by the way, will still offer pleasure in the years to come.

Q: Where can I find a New York State product called Pol Dar Gent Cold Duck?

A: Pol Dar Gent is the brand name of a cold duck wine produced by Manischewitz. When Manischewitz was purchased a few years ago by the Canandaiqua Corporation in New York, the Pol Dar Gent brand was cut back from general distribution. You will have to search for the brand in your area or contact the company. Cold Duck is a sparkling semi-sweet, red wine that was developed and made famous by the old Bronte Winery in Michigan. Cold Duck has lost its marketing appeal and there are only a very few brands still available. Andre and J. Roget are two of the most popular brands that are widely distributed.

Q: Could you please estimate the value of a magnum of Paul Masson California Champagne? The bottle has a seal on its side saying "1964 Highest Award - Official California Wine Judging." Do collectors place ads in any particular publications? Would it be wise to change the cork before contacting a buyer?

A: I am afraid you would be going through a lot of trouble for very little return. First, I doubt the magnum of Paul Masson Champagne has much value to a wine collector. Even if the wine was still drinkable, it does not fall into the super premium category that attracts big money at auctions. Secondly, without a dealer or special license, you can only legally sell your wine collection in Illinois and California. The *Wine Spectator* is one of the most widely distributed wine publications in the United States and does contain a classified section for wine collectors. Unfortunately, your one bottle of a relatively common wine will not create much response. Other than at auctions or charity fundraisers, when people are caught up in the excitement of the event, most private wine transactions involve larger collections of old and rare wines. And finally, although it is recommended to change the corks of rare wines every twenty-five years or so, Champagnes do not usually come under that category because of the difficulty in dealing with a cork under pressure and the fact that sparkling wines do not usually last that long. My best advice to you would be to invite a couple of friends over for a special uncorking of your magnum and share what little pleasure may still be in the wine.

Q: Would a French chateau ship wine to me in the United States?

A: None of the wineries in Europe that I know of will ship an individual wine. I am not even sure that it is legal to do so without a state and/or federal license of some sort. You may bring it back with you as checked baggage, however. You would, of course, have to pay taxes on it as you cleared customs. If you do bring cases of wine back, be sure the winery or shop packs the individual bottles securely in heavy-duty cardboard boxes filled with plenty of styrofoam. If you are considering a relatively large quantity of wine, you could always work through the regular retail and importer channels. I am quite sure it would be easier and probably less expensive in the long run.

Q: How much wine can I bring into the United States from a trip overseas?

A: According to the United States Customs Office, each person is allowed one liter of any alcoholic beverage and a $400 exemption duty-free (five liters and $800, if from the U.S. Virgin Islands). You are allowed to bring in more, but you will be charged 10% duty on your receipts. If you have no receipts, Customs will assign a value. United States Customs will also collect IRS taxes on your additional wine at a rate of 4 cents per liter of still wine, 18 cents per liter on fortified wines (e.g., sherry, liqueurs, etc.) and 90 cents a liter for sparkling wines. Although the 10% duty may still make it attractive to bring in additional bottles of great finds from your trip, the duty rates go up after the first $1,400 ($1,800 from the U.S. Virgin Islands) of all goods purchased overseas. All your purchases must accompany you on your journey, and United States Postal Laws prohibit the shipment of alcoholic beverages by mail. One little kicker: Customs must enforce the liquor laws of the state in which they are operating. The state of California, for example, will allow what Federal Law allows duty-free; 1 liter. If you show up with more, you may not get it cleared or be allowed to pay the extra duty.

Q: Once a cork is pulled from a wine bottle, what should I look for?

A: A simple squeeze of the cork will give a small clue as what to expect in the wine. If it is hard and dry, or crumbly from the corkscrew, the wine may have been stored improperly and may be a sign of poorer quality. If the cork is soft and moist, but not mushy, it's an indication of proper storage. A moldy cork is not necessarily a bad sign. Just wipe off the lip and taste the wine for the true test. By the way, the vast majority of corks come from the trunk bark of cork oak trees grown in Portugal. A much smaller percentage comes from the coast of Southern France, Algeria, Tunisia, Morocco and from the Italian islands of Sardinia, Sicily and Corsica.

Q: Where can I find recipes and information for making my own wines?

A: The best place to start is at your local library or on the internet under wine or home winemaking. The library may also be able to put you in touch with local home winemaking clubs. If you do not have a nearby retail store that sells winemaking kits and supplies, you may wish to contact a local winery. They sometimes sell books and supplies to home winemakers.

Q: Is collecting wine a good investment?

A: By definition, an investment is "money laid out for a profitable return." According to the laws of most states, unless you are a licensed winery, wholesaler or retailer in that state, you cannot buy wine for resale. Obviously, since you have no legal way to make a profit on the money you invested, it would be a bad investment. An exception to this could be donating wine to a charitable fundraiser or non-profit organization and deducting the donation on your tax return at the appreciated fair market value. Better check with your accountant on this, however. The best way to "invest" in wine is to consider your purchase a "hedge against inflation." Premium wines are very susceptible to the laws of supply and demand. If you wish to insure the future availability of a favorite fine wine at today's prices, then an investment of this nature is beneficial.

Q: I have a collection of wines that are kept away from heat, light and vibration and are lying on their sides. Do I have to periodically rotate the bottles as well?

A: No, you are doing just fine. In fact, the less movement of wines in storage the better. You are probably concerned about the accumulation of sediment on the side of the bottle, but don't worry. Sediment is a natural process of wine development and it will not hurt you or the product. It does have a slightly bitter taste, however, and may cause the wine to be cloudy and unattractive. Before serving, you may wish to stand the bottle upright for a few hours to let the sediment settle to the bottom, then carefully decant the wine into a clean carafe, thereby leaving the sediment in the bottle. More important in the storage of fine wines is maintaining a constant temperature under 70°F. Frequent increases or drops in temperature may disrupt the wine's development and cause rapid deterioration.

Q: How can I feel more comfortable ordering wine in a restaurant?

A: *Family Circle* magazine reported on a survey of forty eight New York waiters who "emphatically agreed that drinkers of red wines and white wines have different personality traits." Not only are the former "wild" and "dangerous," the waiters thought, but also "sensual." White wine drinkers were "better dressed," "more chic" and "more cool." Since you are already categorized, no sense in getting flustered about ordering the wrong label. Just relax and order the wine with which you are comfortable. If you have any questions, ask the waiter.

Q: Why is smoking frowned upon at a wine tasting?

A: Like strong perfume and after-shave, smoke will overpower the delicate fragrance and aroma of the wine. But some smokers claim the harshness of smoking makes their taste buds more sensitive to the subtle nuances of the wines. Although wine and smoking is not generally considered a good mixture, Leon D. Adams states in his *Commonsense Book of Wine*, "Red port is the traditional wine to sip while puffing a fragrant cigar. Had it not been for the time honored British custom of after-dinner port for the gentlemen, while the ladies retired from the table, the Portuguese port industry would not be what it is today."

Q: Is it more difficult to visit wineries in Europe or in the United States?

A: It depends on where you want to go. European wineries are not as readily available to the general public as wineries in the United States. Many of the European wineries require appointments, group tours or a letter of introduction from a local distributor or retailer. It is not difficult to make these arrangements. Just ask your local wine merchant to put you in contact with the right people. The United States Trade Commission office in the country you are visiting is another good source of information. In the United States it is usually just a matter of driving up to the winery tasting room during visiting hours to experience the joys of winemaking. The local Chamber of Commerce office, guide books, auto clubs or your travel agent are good sources of help in planning your itinerary.

Q: Can I return a bottle of wine I do not like?

A: You certainly could try, but I do not feel it would be fair to the retailer or restaurant unless it was their specific recommendation. If the wine has turned bad, that would be a different matter. In fact, in many states, the only legal justification for returning alcoholic beverages is if the product is spoiled. If you do not like the style of a wine or purchased more than you need for your party, the store or restaurant should not be asked to bear the cost. Take extra care in your selection and avoid a potentially uncomfortable situation.

Q: I have a friend who will be celebrating his 50th birthday this year. Is it possible to find a bottle of wine from the year of his birth?

A: I have been asked this question hundreds of times and the answer is always the same. If a "birth-date" wine is of high enough quality to last the minimum twenty-one years (the legal age for one to consume wine), then it stands to reason that the economics of supply and demand have set in. There are usually wines of every year available somewhere; the trick is to find them. If you are able to find the vintage you want, it more than likely will be at an inflated price. I would offer two gift alternatives: 1) give the birthday person a selection of unusual wines from around the world, or 2) put away a bottle of wine when it is readily available in retail stores in anticipation of a future birthday, graduation or anniversary. If all else fails, I have yet to see anyone turn down a nice bottle of Champagne for the occasion.

Q: Can I still use my ten year old wine skin?

A: As long as your wine skin does not leak with water in it, it should serve well for any liquid beverage. Before pouring in your wine, however, be sure to rinse the skin thoroughly with warm water. If your wine skin is indeed an animal hide, keep it filled with water for storage and change the water periodically. Many commercial wine skins have a latex liner, which is fine for holding wine for a short while, but has a tendency to give an off-taste to the wine if stored for any lengthy amount of time. Animal hides have been used to store and carry wine, water and other liquid refreshments ever since man found the need for a container that would travel easily.

Q: How can I remove a pressure sensitive wine label from a wine bottle so I may add it to my collection?

A: Try using a good quality, clear plastic tape used for packing. Carefully lay the tape strips over the bottle label, smooth them out and then slowly peel it off. The printed layer of the label should adhere to the tape and separate from the label. Then you can trim the edges and paste it in your label book. There are also some commercial products on the market that are big enough to cover a label with one sheet. These work on the same principle.

Q: I have inherited a 375ml bottle of 1935 Inglenook Cabernet. I am not sure about its storage history and wonder if I should open it or just save it as a conversation piece.

A: Inglenook is a respected name in the Napa Valley, California wine industry. The bottle of Cabernet Sauvignon you have inherited could still be drinkable, but the chances are marginal without a history of how it was stored. Also, the fact that the wine is in a half-bottle speeds up its maturity and reduces the chance that it is still good. Maybe you can have your wine and drink it, too. Carefully remove the bottle capsule and cork so that they may be replaced. If the wine is still good, enjoy. If the wine has turned, recork and reseal it and you still have your conversation piece. Even if the wine is still good, refill the bottle with colored water. The wine would only have value if it were part of a large collection, and storage conditions could be documented. It would be fun to make an event out of opening the wine to find what treasures may reside within.

Q: How can I find out about wine seminars in Germany?

A: The German Wine Academy offers regular courses on wine at all levels of expertise from beginner to professional in both English and German. The Academy is based in a fantastic 12th century monastery in the Rheingau. The courses include tastings and tours through the German wine regions. For more particulars, write to: The German Wine Academy, P.O. Box 1795, D-6500 Mainz, West Germany.

Q: If my home state forbids it, where can I legally sell my wine collections?

A: How about Chicago, New York, or Los Angeles? As the top three wine markets in the country the auction houses of Christie's, Sotheby's, Chicago Wine Company and others, do big business in vintage wine sales. Their commissions will run anywhere from 15 to 35 percent of the selling price. Obviously, there has to be plenty of appreciation between your original purchase price and the current market price. There are a number of legal charity wine auctions that allow donations from your collection. You may then be eligible for a federal or state tax deduction or, in some cases, a tax credit.

Q: What are the career possibilities in the wine industry?

A: There are a number of career areas to pursue in the wine industry. The easiest to enter without extensive courses in chemistry, biology or horticulture is marketing. If you have a background in retail wine sales, it would give you good experience for representing a winery or wholesale distributor. If winemaking is your objective, I am afraid there are no shortcuts. Most winemakers have extensive formal training or started as amateur winemakers and gained experience over a number of years of trial and error. Even for hobbyists, winemaking today is quite involved.

Technical knowledge and study in the sciences is necessary to be commercially successful. That does not rule out the possibility of finding an entry level position at a winery and learning the production business while you complete formal study. A sales background is still your best bet. In wine sales you will have access to a number of inside information sources and you can acquire hands-on knowledge about amateur winemaking. At least while you are gathering the "know how," you will also be able to support yourself and still remain in the wine industry.

Q: Is it legal to buy wine to go from a restaurant? What about an unfinished bottle from dinner?

A: There are different laws governing the use and sale of liquor in each of the fifty states. In general, however, some restaurants do have a retail take-out license from local State Liquor Control Agencies, as well as the primary license to serve alcoholic beverages, the most common license obtained by restaurants. In most cases, the take-out license must be applied for separately. In some states it is a violation for a licensed restaurant to allow patrons to bring in their own wine. In these states, wine must be purchased from the licensee. With regard to an unfinished bottle, in most states it is not legal for the restaurant to allow an opened bottle of wine to leave the premises. Local and state police also take a dim view of finding a half-consumed bottle of wine in your car. For more definitive answers regarding the sale and use of alcoholic beverages, contact your local State Liquor Control Agency.

Q: Does the size of the bottle have an affect on the taste of the wine?

A: Yes, indeed. In general, the bigger the bottle the better the wine will keep. Wine has a constantly changing natural life span and the effective length of life, speed of maturity and level of ultimate quality are all in direct proportion to bottle size. Half-bottles are designed primarily for the restaurant trade where it is a convenient portion size for dining patrons. I would suggest full (750ml) bottles or better yet, magnum (1.5L) bottles, for future purchases for your collection.

Q: What is your recommendation for building a home wine cellar?

A: Wine cellars can be as elaborate as your checkbook allows or as simple as a storage closet. The important thing to remember is that wine should be stored in an area that is free of vibration, does not encounter direct sunlight and has a relatively constant cool temperature. If you anticipate a large investment in wine to be stored over a number of years, then a professionally built cellar may be in order. Storage of rare vintage wines should be in a controlled temperature of around 55 to 60°F. Storage racks, of just about any material, should be designed to fit the available space and accommodate wine bottles that are stored on their sides to keep the corks moist. The ideal situation for the long-term storage of fine, rare wines is an air-conditioned room built on the outside foundation of the home and insulated sufficiently to keep out the influences of the home's heat-producing units. For shorter time storage (under two years), a simple enclosed area where the temperature does not vary more than ten degrees from 60°F at any time will work well for a constantly changing inventory. For more detailed information consult professional builders of saunas and wine vaults or wine reference books that give instructions and layouts of wine storage areas.

Q: Is it best to store wine bottles in round clay tiles?

A: The tiles work well if you have the room. Since they take up a lot of valuable storage space, I would suggest storing six to twelve wine bottles on top of each other in sections partitioned by wood. This is the most efficient use of space and it allows air circulation around the glass bottles which is the most important factor in keeping all the bottles cool.

Q: In the early 1930s my father was given a bottle of ruby port from Douro, Oporto, Portugal. Is it of any value and would it still be good?

A: It is quite possible that your bottle is still palatable, even though its monetary value is minimal. By Portuguese law, *Porto* is the designated wine from the Upper Douro River region. This red wine is fortified by the addition of Portuguese brandy and shipped from Oporto, the city at the mouth of the Douro that gave the port its name. Made world-famous by British connoisseurs, Vintage *Porto* has been known to age for decades and, indeed, centuries. Unfortunately, Ruby Port is a slightly inferior *Porto* rich in color, fruity and sweet early in its life. Ruby Port is a blend of the wines of several years and does not improve much in the bottle.

Q: How do I keep wine left over from dinner from going bad?

A: Once wine has been opened and exposed to oxygen, it begins to deteriorate. If you were to recork the bottle and place it in the refrigerator, it should delay the deterioration process for a few days. It will be drinkable, but not exactly as it was originally at the dinner table. If you purchase wine in large containers and decant it into smaller, capped bottles, the wine should be suitable for leisurely serving later without losing much quality. There are also a number of reliable products on the market like "Vacu Vin" that remove the oxygen in the bottle or replace it with nitrogen for temporary storage.

Q: What elements should one look for in evaluating a quality wine?

A: First and foremost, the wine must be free of defects such as off-odors and tastes. The color should be clear and brilliant. If the wine is appealing to the eye, it signals our other senses of taste and smell to be prepared for a pleasing experience. The fragrance of wine is as important as flavor, since our nose, more than anything else, influences our sense of taste. In a truly fine quality wine, flavors should be complex and produce different taste sensations with each smell or sip. Yet, the flavors should be balanced. If the wine is sweet, it should be offset with acidity or it will taste flat. If it is dry, there should be no harshness and the wine must have body and substance. Otherwise, it will appear thin and watery. Young wines should have full fruit flavor and aroma while older wines entice with intriguing nuances from barrel or bottle aging. Above all else, a wine must be pleasing to your individual taste.

Q: How can I avoid frustration with poor restaurant service?

A: A few years ago I read an article by Anthony Dias Blue in which he introduced his "Diner's Bill of Rights." Since we have all experienced various forms of dissatisfaction in a restaurant, I compiled some of Mr. Blue's ideas, plus my own viewpoints, and present them here as "A Culinary Emancipation Proclamation."

Proclamation #1. The guest shall have the right to expect a table within a reasonable time from the agreed-upon reservation time.

I have no problem with a cocktail in the lounge for a 15 minute wait while the table is being cleared and reset, but an hour or more is unacceptable. Establishments that are overbooking should be prepared to suffer the inevitable consequence of dissatisfied guests. We do, however, relinquish this right if we are so inconsiderate as to not arrive at the reserved time.

Proclamation #2. The diner has the right to expect that what is being served is what was ordered.

Ever been served a cut or quality of meat that differed from what you ordered, by someone who apparently figured you would not know the difference? Or how about the situation in which you order a traditional entrée from the menu and are served some concoction you never knew was possible? I don't appreciate being conned by a switch artist in the kitchen. If the chef adds a personal touch to a traditional dish, I prefer to be forewarned. If I want surprises, I will order the leftover special.

Proclamation #3. The guest has the right to expect consistency in a restaurant.

As in any business, this is a basic management problem. All chefs, cooks, service people and bartenders should be trained from the same "hymn book." Nothing is more disheartening than to discover a real restaurant gem, then return with friends the following week, only to be treated to an elaborate disaster.

Proclamation #4. The guest shall have the right to return dishes to the kitchen for reasonable cause.

The key phrase here is "reasonable cause." In other words, food that is cold, spoiled, prepared differently then what was ordered, or not what was ordered at all. Just because you do not like the taste may not be sufficient cause; the restaurant is well within its right to bill you for the meal. This right of refusal is canceled, however, if it is not exercised after the first few bites. If the food is good enough half way through, it is good enough all the way through.

Proclamation #5. The guest has the right to have the wine opened at the table and poured into glasses larger than giant thimbles.

Obviously, presenting a guest with an unopened bottle of wine assures that which is ordered is also served. When wine is uncorked at the table, the possibility of substituting a Mongolian burgundy for the $200 Chateau Lafite is eliminated. As for the stemware in which it is served, part of the enjoyment and romance of wine is swirling and inhaling the fragrance. That requires an 8 to 10 ounce glass, not a 4 or 5 ounce thimble filled to the top. As in the previous proclamation, we also have the right to reject a bad bottle of wine. Notice I said "bad" and not "don't like." Just because you do not like the particular bottle you ordered is no fault of the restaurant. On the other hand, you are not responsible for bad storage or mishandling that causes a corky smell and taste or spoilage of the wine. Establish that you know what you are talking about and do not be intimidated.

Proclamation #6. The guest has the right to a correctly totaled and legible check.

Never assume the bottom line is correct without checking it first. I cannot tell you the number of times I have found that 1 and 1 add up to 3 — or that all the scribbling included two desserts from the next table. Even those computer registers have a tendency to repeat an item occasionally.

Proclamation #7. The guest has the right to undertip or not tip at all if the service is poor.

Contrary to the viewpoints of some service people who think they have an inherent right to be tipped a full twenty percent, tipping is still a reward for a job well done. Tip according to the service you have received, under tip for unsatisfactory service and leave more for exceptional service. Do not be intimidated by arrogant servers; if you get some verbal abuse, just explain why the gratuity is less than normal.

Proclamation #8. The guest pledges to be fair and willing to give management the opportunity to correct any unsatisfactory service.

If, however, an establishment continues to treat guests poorly, serves bad food or wine, and does not offer to make restitution for shoddy service and inferior product brought to its attention, then fight back with the ultimate weapon. Do not go back!...and go forth into the world and spread the word.

Wine in General

It is the unbroken testimony of all history
that alcoholic liquors have been used by the
strongest, wisest, handsomest,
and in every way,
the best races of all times.

GEORGE SAINTSBURY

•

If you like it — drink it!
Don't let anyone intimidate you.
You are the best judge of your
taste preferences.

JOE BORRELLO

Q: Will wines made in the United States ever achieve the greatness of European wines?

A: Some people feel that they already have, in some cases. In my opinion, wines made in this country are as good as most throughout the world. The super premium wines of the great first-growths in France, however, are still the best wines on earth. Given the centuries of winemaking in France compared to this country's advances made over a much shorter period of time, I would dare to venture that United States technology will duplicate or surpass the best of European winemaking within the next few decades.

Q: How many states produce wine commercially?

A: According to the December 2001 Buyers Guide from *Wines & Vines Magazine* (the people who keep track of those kinds of things), the only state that does not have a commercial winery is North Dakota. And yes, there are BATF bonded wineries in Alaska and Hawaii.

Q: What is meant by a wine's appellation?

A: An appellation is a government-designated grape-growing area that possesses distinct climate, soil and overall growing conditions that are unique from other agricultural regions.

The most famous wine appellation designations are those governed by the *Appellation Contrôlée* laws of France. They go beyond growing conditions and land areas to the point of restricting grape varieties and the amount of tonnage to be harvested per hectare. It must be noted, however, that although the French government strictly enforces *Appellation Contrôlée* regulations, it does not necessarily guarantee quality — only the grape's origin and compliance with the restrictions delegated to that particular region.

In the United States, an appellation (or "Approved Viticultural Area," or an AVA) is assigned only to a growing region that has proven to the Bureau of Alcohol, Tobacco and Firearms (BATF) that it has unique growing capabilities. An AVA also has a tendency to follow political borders. For example, Napa Valley and Sonoma County are designated AVA's. Again, quality is not guaranteed — only that at least 85% of the grapes used to make a particular wine were grown in the appellation area indicated on the bottle label.

AVA's are as concentrated as "Russian River" and as broad as "American," which means grapes from anywhere in the country were used to produce the wine. The problem with the American Appellation is that the wine does not portray any unique characteristics of a single growing district. Grapes from California, Washington and New York may be blended together to make wine under an American Appellation. This happens often during years of low-yielding harvests. There is nothing wrong with the wine, it is just difficult to market the product under such a generic and nondistinctive appellation.

Q: What does the term *mis en bouteilles au chateau* mean on the label of my wine bottles?

A: When a French wine is bottled on the property that grew the grapes and produced the wine, it may be labeled *mis en bouteilles au chateau,* or "bottled at the Chateau." In the United States the term estate-bottled is used under the same conditions. Chateau or estate bottling is practiced by the vast majority of better vineyards around the world. It is a guarantee of authenticity, but not necessarily one of quality. The earned reputation of the winery and your individual palate are still the best criteria for judging a wine's merit.

Q: There must be some really big money to be made in the wine business with so many fantastic chateau estates in France. Is it as glamorous as it seems?

A: In the wine trade a chateau is not necessarily a great castle. It is more often merely a country house which serves as the center of activity in the vineyards and a collection of sheds and barns, much like you would find on any farm. There are, indeed, many grand chateaux, however, particularly in the Loire Valley. Most of these magnificent buildings were built generations ago with family wealth obtained by other means. Vineyards were merely a hobby for many rich aristocrats who obviously never worked the land themselves. Today, it is very costly to begin a vineyard anywhere in the world due to the high costs of land and labor. Because of the tremendous demand in time and money, the making of wine has become a very serious and risky business. There is a saying in the trade that states, "If you want to make a small fortune in the wine business, you must start with a large fortune!"

Q: What would you consider the best all around wine?

A: I don't believe there is such a thing. Not only do tastes differ, but so does the natural chemistry of food and wine. At the risk of sounding evasive, the best advice still is to experiment with different wine and food combinations. Develop your own favorites and all around wine to meet your lifestyle. That's the beauty and fun of wine and food.

Q: What are D.I. wines?

A: D.I. stands for Direct Import. Wine merchants have made a commitment to purchase a certain amount of wine directly from the winery at discount prices. The reason for the discount is the merchant bought enough volume, either by himself or with other merchants, to allow the importer to charge a discounted fee for handling the paperwork. The merchant is usually required to take delivery immediately. This also means the merchant must pay for it within a very short period of time. Obviously, he does not want a hundred or more cases of any particular wine sitting around gathering dust and affecting cash flow. Usually D.I. wines are very good values that have been personally selected by the merchant. Try a bottle first, then go back and negotiate case prices if you think you've come upon a find. By the way, D.I.s do not just come from overseas. Many United States wineries are now using this sales tactic as well.

Q: What are wine futures?

A: Like many other consumable products affected by the laws of supply and demand, the purchase of fine wines at lower prices may be considered even before release to the general public. This is called "buying in wine futures" and can be a very risky business for the uninformed. Each year at the conclusion of harvest, many top premium wineries and estates will offer a limited amount of their new vintage wine at an established price payable in advance, but delivered one to three years in the future. Since the commitment to purchase these wines is made well in advance of their maturity, you must either have an extremely well-educated palate or a lot of trust in someone else's opinion and knowledge of the wine. Depending on the wine's development and international dollar valuation at the time of release, you may or may not have made a good purchase. Wine futures are usually available through specialty wine shops.

Q: What is the difference between wines labeled "non-alcoholic" and those marked "de-alcoholized?"

A: Bottles labeled non-alcoholic without the word wine on the label are usually only fruit juices that have not been fermented into wine. De-alcoholized products began as actual wines and the alcohol was then removed by either a heat or filtering process. Since the non-alcoholic juices have never gone through the winemaking process they are usually much less expensive than the more involved de-alcoholized wines. However, the juices are usually sweeter and do not have the taste of a finished wine. Sparkling, non-alcoholic juices are currently very popular items in local grocery stores, while de-alcoholized wine is still in the developmental stages.

Q: What is a blind tasting?

A: Many people have a tendency to judge a wine by its label. If the wine variety and producer is well known, the chances are it will do well in a comparative wine tasting against a lesser known wine. The best way to get honest evaluations in a comparative tasting is to cover the labels so they cannot be identified and influence opinions. When identities are unknown before a wine tasting, it is considered a blind tasting. Almost all wine judgings and competitions require the tasting to be blind, and identities are never known until the very end of the event. Blind tastings are also a favorite form of private tasting for winemakers. By not knowing the wine's identity, they can make unbiased evaluations on how their wines compare to the competition.

Q: How do you organize and conduct a wine auction for a charity?

A: Your best source would be a local wine merchant. The wine merchant could help you plan and put together an event, as well as serve as a contact for wholesalers, wineries and restaurants who may wish to participate.

You will need a mailing list of people who are supporters of your organization to recruit volunteers and for invitations. Your local media would also be a valuable contact to help promote the event. They may even wish to participate as a co-sponsor and help underwrite some of the promotional costs. There are many organizational details such as glasses, room availability, invitations, programs, food, etc. that must be taken care of. These are best handled by a formal committee of volunteers. Also, there are some legal restrictions and you may have to obtain a special twenty-four hour "auction license" from your local Liquor Control Agency.

Q: What causes leakage in a stored wine bottle?

A: These bottles are commonly called "leakers" at the winery and are usually pulled and consumed at the winemaker's table or in the tasting room. Upon occasion a leaker gets labeled and out into the system. It is simply a fault in the makeup or size of the cork. In either case, if you are comfortable with your local wine merchant, you could take it back for a sealed bottle. Or, open it and enjoy it tonight.

Q: Before corks were discovered, what was used to seal the wine from the air?

A: A layer of olive oil was commonly used to seal the mouth of the clay storage jar called *amphora*. This technique was used for centuries before the invention of both the cork and the bottle, which happened around the same time.

Q: With rising concerns about cork shortages, why aren't more cork trees planted?

A: The problem lies with the fact that a cork tree is recommended to attain at least thirty years of age in order for its bark to be considered for premium corks. Once the tree is stripped of its cork, it takes an additional 7-10 years for the tree to replace bark suitable for harvesting wine corks. A cork tree will have an average of fifteen harvests in its lifetime.

Q: Do those commercial wine preserver devices really work for partially used bottles of wine?

A: They are the next best thing to an unopened bottle of wine and they help delay wine going bad once the bottle is opened. The most popular systems utilize one of two methods, either the "nitrogen replacement" system or the "vacuum" method. With the nitrogen system, oxygen, which contributes to the deterioration of the wine, is replaced with nitrogen from an attached canister and enters the bottle as wine is removed. System costs range from $75 to hundreds of dollars when cabinets are added. Wine bars and restaurants utilize these systems in order to offer a greater variety of fine wines by the glass to customers. For home use the vacuum system is more practical and nearly as effective. For under $25 you get an easy-to-use device that draws out the air and creates a vacuum in the bottle to preserve the remaining wine. In both cases, however, the wine will eventually spoil, but the devices are definitely effective in preserving wine for a much longer period of time than merely placing the cork back in the bottle.

Q: Is there any such thing as a perfect wine glass?

A: Only if it is practical, clear and clean. I personally prefer either bowl or tulip shaped, eight to ten ounce glasses for enjoying wine. This size allows the wine to be swirled and releases its bouquet, providing it is not filled more than half full. A fresh glass for each new wine is recommended so the flavors do not blend together.

Q: Is it true that white wine is made from white or green grapes and red wine is made from red or black grapes?

A: The juice of virtually all grapes is clear. The color of wine actually comes from the grape skins when they are in contact with the juice during the annual crush. This mixture of grape pulp and skin mixture is called the must. During early fermentation, red wine derives its color, body and other natural properties that determine the quality of the finished product from the must. Eventually, the must is filtered away from the wine juice and discarded. If the skins are not allowed to come in contact with the juice, the result will be a white wine. The best example of white wine from black grapes is Pinot Noir which has been used for centuries in the making of premium Champagnes.

Q: Who is at fault when a bottle of wine goes bad?

A: Take your pick: The winery, the importer, the local distributor, the restaurant, retailer or you. The same principles of protecting wine from excessive vibration, widespread heat variation and overexposure to light apply to all who handle the wine. When anyone in the chain is careless with storage or handling of this perishable commodity, nature revolts. Sometimes Mother Nature just has a bad day and picks on you to witness her wrath by messing up the wine's chemistry in the bottle. If you have done your part in protecting the wine, take it back to the place where you bought it. Most reputable merchants will not hesitate to replace it.

Q: What type of information should I expect to get from a wine bottle label?

A: All wine labels are required to give you the following information:

- The brand name of the wine.
- The type of wine. This name may be simply the marketing name of a blended wine, or the name of the grape variety which indicates the wine is made of at least 75% of the variety indicated.
- The Region or Origin. To say "California," 75% of the grapes used to make the wine must be grown within the state. To use a federally approved viticultural area like "Napa Valley," 85% of the grapes must be grown within that area. If a specific vineyard is indicated, 95% of the wine must be made from grapes from that particular vineyard.
- Bottler. The name and location of the bottler must appear on the label. The bottler's name may not always be the same as the brand name.
- Alcohol Content. The legal limits for table wine are between 7% and 14%. The term "table wine" may appear instead of the actual percentage.
- Vintage. If the vintner decides to show a vintage date on the label, the wine must contain 95% of the grapes grown in the year stated.
- Specific character. Several terms may be used to describe method, color, sweetness or other qualities, e.g. Late Harvest, *Demi-Sec,* Dry White, Extra-Dry, etc.

Q: Why are prices of wine so much higher in restaurants than in the retail stores?

A: Restaurant overhead expenses are the biggest culprits, although some establishments go beyond what is reasonable. Service, linen, décor, glassware, entertainment, etc. are all costs unique to the restaurant business and must be recouped in the menu prices. Two (for expensive wines) or three (for inexpensive wines) times wholesale cost is a reasonable mark-up for restaurants. In my opinion, the three to five times cost is out of line and will cost the restaurant business in the long run. Many managers do not realize that customers have no price reference for *cotelettes de veau marquise* on the entrée menu, but do know that the bottle of Macon Villages listed at $40 on the wine list is also available at the corner wine shop for under $15. Astute restaurateurs have learned that smaller mark-ups on wine encourage increased sales and higher dollar profits. Others are still wondering why they do not sell more wine in their establishments. They may never see the light, even after guests have long abandoned them.

Q: What are the factors that make some wines achieve values of $10,000 or more at a wine auction?

A: Simple supply and demand. Like any rare collectable, there is a certain attraction for some people to own what others cannot have or afford. Of course, if you are in the wine or food business, the publicity does not hurt either. With the media coverage of these wine auctions, $10,000 would not begin to pay for the free exposure these entrepreneurs obtain. The one kicker in all the heated excitement of a rare vintage wine auction is that there is no guarantee the wine is still drinkable. Buying wine is much less risky and much more inexpensive at your local wine store. By the way, William Sokolin paid $519,750.00 for a bottle of 1787 vintage wine a few years ago, which supposedly had been owned by Thomas Jefferson. While showing off his prized possession he accidentally knocked it over, breaking it and spilling the precious contents on the floor. Now that is pain few of us will ever experience.

Q: What is meant by a well-balanced wine?

A: When the desirable elements of sugar, acid, flavor and alcohol are in appropriately pleasing proportions, we have a well-balanced wine. Obviously, this leaves the door open to personal taste and preference.

Q: How much wine is contained in some of those larger sized bottles?

A: Historically, wine has been bottled and distributed in the classic 750 milliliter wine bottle. This tapered-neck container has become familiar to everyone who has ordered a bottle of wine at a restaurant or drawn a wine cork in the comfort of their home. Of late, some of the oversize wine bottles have been surfacing in retail stores and at benefit auctions as novelty items for collectors. These larger bottles are usually released in limited numbers, but have been used by European wineries for centuries. The following table may help to sort out any confusion and, incidentally, help you to determine whether that Jeroboam is really less expensive than four individual bottles.

Size	Number of Bottles	Milliliters	Liters	Ounces
Bottle	1	750	0.75	26
Magnum	2	1500	1.5	52
Jeroboam	4	3000	3.0	104
Rehoboam	6	4500	4.5	156
Methuselah	8	6000	6.0	208
Salmanazar	12	9000	9.0	312
Balthazar	16	12000	12	416
Nebuchadnezzar	20	15000	15	520

Q: What percentage of American wine is consumed by Americans?

A: Nearly 80% of the wine consumed by Americans is produced in this country. Yet, that production represents less than 10% of the world's total harvest. Only 41% of United States grape production is made into wine, however, so there's plenty of room for growth.

Q: What would be the ratio of soft drink consumption to wine consumption in the United States?

A: According to the United States Department of Agriculture's statistics released in the late 1990s, Americans consume annually over 53 gallons of soft drinks, 23.5 gallons of coffee and 22 gallons of beer per person. Compare that with personal consumption of just two gallons of wine and you have close to a 30 to 1 ratio of soft drinks to wine. The French and Italians consume 15-plus gallons of wine per year and the beer-loving British drink eight gallons of wine annually.

Q: Some wines have a musty smell. What causes this?

A: The musty smell you have detected is the result of a chemical called trichloroanisole (TCA). The so-called "corked" or "corky" wine has a moldy odor as the result of an interaction of mold, chlorine and phenols (organic compounds found in all plants). Australian researchers have found that as many as two percent of wine bottles may be affected by cork taint. Of course, the wineries say it is the result of defective corks and the cork manufacturers claim it is something in the bottle-sterilization process that causes the problem. The truth is, nobody knows for sure, but everyone admits it does happen on occasion. TCA can develop in the forest, during the cork production process, in wine bottles, cardboard cases, wooden palettes or during storage at the winery. When you do encounter a corked wine, and it is an easily recognizable odor, either return the bottle to the merchant you purchased it from or ask your restaurant server to replace it. If either place is reputable, you should not have any trouble. To avoid the problem at a home dinner party, do what many collectors do and buy two or more bottles of each wine. Since corked bottles are usually isolated instances, you will always have a backup bottle.

Q: Since wine corks are porous and natural products, do they eventually decay and break down?

A: Corks will indeed decay and disintegrate, leaving the wine with no protection from harmful oxygen. Many wineries that keep an inventory of older wines have a program where they periodically "recork" bottles and "top off" evaporated wine. The usual time to recork bottles is around the wine's 25th birthday. If you are a serious collector, you may want to consider the same practice, especially if you notice bottles beginning to leak out the top or the cork crumbles under the pressure of the corkscrew.

Q: How do you get a broken cork out of the bottle?

A: I assume you already tried to reuse the corkscrew and found that the cork crumbled or was pushed further into the bottle. If it crumbled, clean out the loose pieces and push what is left of the cork into the bottle. At least now the wine can be poured. There are two ways to handle the pesky cork. The easiest way would be to carefully decant the wine into a clean decanter bottle and serve. If you are determined to serve from the bottle, and have no other glass receptacle or a commercial cork retriever, then you must be a little more resourceful. Take a piece of sturdy string and tie a double or triple knot at the end. Lower the string, knot first, into the wine so it drops below the floating cork. Now maneuver the string so that the knot will wedge against the bottle and the bottom of the cork, which is now facing up toward the bottle neck opening. Slowing pull up on the string, using the knot as leverage to force the cork up and out. Obviously, this little trick will not work on a bottle of wine that is partially empty. Your only choice then is to pour the wine and not worry about the cork.

Q: What is a tastevin?

A: Tastevin (taht-van) is part of the pomp and circumstance of wine presentation that a restaurant may wish to express. The tastevin is simply a shallow tasting cup for the wine steward or *sommelier* to sample the wine before serving it at your table. The cup is usually silver lined with little nubs or indentations on the bottom. The silver does not impart an off-taste and is easily kept clean. The indentations are intended to reflect the light so the color may be examined by the wine steward. It is one of those showbiz props that are more decorative than necessary, but some find it entertaining.

Q: Why does the subject of wine have so much appeal?

A: Wine has a certain mystique that entices the curiosity and desire in the general public. I once read, "Wine, given the right combination of grapes, weather, aging and winemaker ability, is often as complex a commodity as an alluring painting, a compelling novel or a synchronized symphony. It is more than just another food or beverage. Wine is as much an art form as it is a scientific phenomena and an agricultural product. The more one learns about this alluring subject, the more enjoyment and appreciation is derived from its experiences. Wine is versatile and all giving, from an unassuming companion with a meal to a position of cultural significance and social status. As with many other art forms, man has created a love affair with wine as an extension of his desire to intermingle and become one with all that is natural and reaches the soul." A wonderfully written explanation and I apologize to the author for not knowing who to give the literary credit.

Q: What is an estate bottled wine?

A: For wine bottled in the United States after 1982, this term may be used on the label only if "the wine bears a delimited viticultural area place of origin and the bottling winery (1) is located in that area, (2) grew all of the grapes used to make the wine on land owned or controlled by the winery within that area and (3) crushed the grapes, fermented the resulting must and finished, aged and bottled the wine in a continuous process, the wine at no time having left the premises of the bottling winery." Estate bottled usually alludes to a premium wine, but is no guarantee of quality.

Q: What does the acronym BATF stand for?

A: BATF stands for Bureau of Alcohol, Tobacco and Firearms. This is the Federal agency that regulates trade and collects United States taxes on items named in their title. The agency is part of the Treasury Department.

Q: Does the term table wine on a wine label have any special meaning about the quality of the wine?

A: Table wine is designated by the Bureau of Alcohol, Tobacco and Firearms as a grape wine with 14% or less alcohol. The lower limit is 7%. Wines with over 14% alcohol, but less than 21% are classed as dessert or fortified wines, whether they are sweet or dry. The designations are for the purpose of determining federal and state taxes more than anything else. Products over 21% alcohol content fall into the categories of liquor or liqueurs.

Q: Is there a special wine used for communion services and is it available commercially?

A: According to various religious officials we have contacted, the church hierarchy does not specify any particular wine for use at communion. The choice of wine is usually left to the discretion of the pastor or church committee and is generally commercially available. Further investigation shows that the popular choices of various denominations include New York Concord and Niagara wines, California bulk wines and other mellow, semi-sweet wines all usually available from your retail store. Ask your local clergy for more specific information about what is used in your church.

Q: How do professionals judge wines in competition and award medals?

A: All competitions have different methods, but a good guideline is the one used by Tasters Guild International in their annual wine evaluation. To be fair and unbiased, the wines are always tasted blind (the labels of the wines are not exposed until after they have been evaluated). Only the variety of the grapes, vintage year, degree of sweetness, and price category are made known to the tasters to evaluate the quality of the wine, the skill of the winemaker and the perceived consumer value of the product. The actual evaluation of the wines is based on a cumulative twenty-point system. First, using a clear, stemmed glass, the wine is examined as to the clarity of color. Is it cloudy or clear? Is the color correct for the type of wine being evaluated? Various grape varieties produce diverse color hues and tones (0-2 points awarded). Next, is the sense of smell. The grape variety used should be recognizable by the fragrance or aroma (0-2 points awarded). The bouquet is slightly different from aroma and is the result of proper fermentation, handling and aging of the wine with its many complex factors intertwined (0-2 points awarded). Sensitive taste buds will detect the wine's natural acid content. If there is too much acid, the wine will be very tart and sour, if there is too little, the wine will be flat and flabby (0-2 points awarded). The wine's acid must balance with sugar content to achieve the desired clean, crisp taste of fruit essence (0-2 points awarded). There should also be a desired complexity in the makeup of wine, yet the taste should have a distinct flavor of the grape variety and balance with the fruit aroma (0-3 points awarded). In the case of red wines, the wine should have a slight astringency, much like the puckering effect of lemon juice (0-1 point awarded). This is the result of tannin, which allows the wine to age properly. Up to two additional points are allowed for the body or feel of the wine within the mouth. There should be the obvious presence of substance or density on the palate as opposed to being thin and watery. Finally, personal judgment and experience makes the conclusive assessment as to the overall general quality of the wine by the pleasant lingering finish that says it is all in perfect harmony (0-4 points awarded). When the scores are tallied, 18-20 earns a gold, 16-17.9 is awarded a silver and 14-15.9 receives the bronze.

Q: In a wine judging, how can your body tolerate that much wine consumption and still remain objective in your evaluations?

A: Before you come to the conclusion that at the end of a day of wine tasting the judges have all they can do to walk a straight line, let me assure you nothing of the kind happens. The concentration and perception of the senses is so intense that it is paramount that one remains in complete control of his or her faculties. Indeed, in most cases, the judges do not swallow the wine. It is not necessary to swallow to evaluate how the wine affects the senses of taste, smell, sight and feel. To clear and case the palate, water and plain bread are consumed after every wine. Although much of the wine is not consumed, six hours of evaluating does take its toll. I have overheard a first-time judge exclaim, "I feel like I've just played five sets of tennis."

Legends and Myths

One barrel of wine can work more miracles
than a church full of saints.

AN OLD ITALIAN PROVERB

•

If there's a story behind the wine,
I enjoy it even more.

JOE BORRELLO

Q: Who is credited with the discovery of wine, the Greeks or the Romans?

A: The story of wine starts even before either of these two great cultures came on to the scene. Evidence of wine accompanies some of the earliest accounts of the actual development of civilized man. However, the most prominent historical evidence of man's love for wine is supplied by the Greeks around 1000 BC. It was from this point that wine became deeply entrenched in man's culture, thanks mainly to the expansion of the Greek and Roman Empires throughout Europe and Northern Africa. History seems to indicate that the Romans were the most prolific perpetrators of the vine, especially with their introduction to Gaul. By the time the Romans left what we now know as France in the fifth century, they had laid the foundations for almost all the greatest vineyards of the modern world. As a side note, it is interesting that the early Vikings called America "Vinland" because of all the native grape vines they found in their explorations — centuries before the arrival of Columbus.

Q: Is it true that if it were not for the Catholic Church and the monks of the Middle Ages we would not even have wine today?

A: I am not sure I would go quite that far, but the Catholic Church, through its monasteries, was certainly instrumental in preserving, teaching and developing the techniques of winemaking through the Dark Ages. Indeed, the Church was one of the leading landowners and for centuries owned many of the greatest vineyards of Europe. Monks of the monasteries cleared hillsides and developed the land bequeathed to the Church by dying wine-growers. In a time when man's progress stood relatively still, the styles of wine familiar to us today were guided by the efforts of the Church. There seems to be some truth to the statement by Benjamin Franklin, who said, "Wine is a constant proof that God loves us and likes to see us happy!"

Q: How does the term honeymoon have its origin in wines?

A: In ancient Babylon, the bride's father would supply his son-in-law with all the mead (fermented honey beverage) he could drink for a month after the wedding. Because the early calendar was lunar, or moon-based, this period of free mead was called the "honey month," or what we now call the honeymoon. Sounds palatable to me.

Q: How long have connoisseurs been enjoying quality wines?

A: The first known reference to a specific wine vintage was made by Roman historian Pliny the Elder, who rated the 121 B.C. vintage as one "of the highest in excellence." Pliny noted how well it had lasted over its 200 years of age. Just a little south of Rome, archeologists have uncovered and identified over 200 wine bars in the volcanic ruins of Pompeii. It would seem that mankind has been enjoying the fruit of the vine for some time.

Q: What is the name of the man who is considered the "Father of the California wine industry?" Isn't there also an individual who was instrumental in developing European vines in the East, as well?

A: The Hungarian Agoston Haraszthy is considered to have prompted the "Wine Rush" in California with his plantings of scores of new vine varieties in the 1840s. Dr. Konstantin Frank is the gentleman who proved that good wine could be made from European vinifera grapes in New York's Finger Lakes district. That philosophy has spread throughout the East and the Midwest and is continuing to develop.

Q: Is it true that author Ernest Hemingway so loved a particular wine that he named one of his children after it?

A: It is true that Hemingway was extremely fond of the exceptional wines of Chateau Margaux in the Haut-Medoc region of Bordeaux, France. And his actress/granddaughter (Hemingway's offspring were all male) does indeed bear the name of Margaux, the French version of Margaret. The story persists within wine pubs and the trade that Margaux Hemingway was named in tribute to her grandfather's well-known passion for the wine of the famous "First Growth" estate.

Q: I witnessed a strange sight and hopefully you can enlighten me. A hot air balloon landed in a field near my home and a person got out of the basket, opened a bottle of Champagne, poured it on the ground and proceeded to make a mud pie. What was going on?

A: According to my ballooning friends, you watched the landing of a pilot's first solo flight. It is a tradition that started in France (where ballooning also started) and has spread throughout the ballooning world. The mud pie was for the purpose of recording the date of the feat. Along with the pilot's initials, it makes a unique paperweight memento when it hardens. Obviously, since it is a French tradition, Champagne is the wine of choice for the commemoration.

Q: Please give me information on what the following wines are worth today: a 3-liter bottle of 1959 Bardi Chianti, 1936 California Sparkling Burgundy and 1936 New York Champagne.

A: Unfortunately, it is a common misnomer that any wine old enough will eventually be worth a lot of money. In reality, less than 1% of the world's wine production lasts longer than 10-15 years, let alone become a collector's item. I am afraid your wines are only valuable as conversation pieces or as attractions for antique bottle collectors. The contents of the bottles probably lost their luster long ago.

Q: In Italy I was served Sambuca after dinner with coffee beans in it. What is the significance of the beans?

A: Tradition calls for Sambuca, an after-dinner liqueur, to be served with an odd number of espresso beans (usually three or five) placed in a glass for good luck. The flavors of the coffee beans and the anisette-flavored liqueur are a natural taste combination. However, never accept a glass of Sambuca with an even number of beans — I do not know what would happen, but I have seen bartenders in Rome go berserk when they saw a glass go to a guest with only two beans. Do not take the chance, especially in Rome!

Q: I know the Greeks and Romans were most responsible for the development of wine, but what about whisky? Where did it come from?

A: Legend has it that the secrets of distilling came to Scotland from Ireland, and that it was introduced there by St. Patrick around 400 A.D. He had traveled on the Continent and may have learned about distilling there. However, it is not certain whether anyone in Europe knew how to distill until 500 years later. It is known, however, that distilling was first done in monasteries, to produce medicine. Irish records make note of this in the late 1100s, and the earliest Scottish record — in the Royal Exchequer Rolls of 1494 — is of the sale of 500 kgs (1,120 pounds) of malt to one Friar John Corr "wherewith to make *aqua vitae*" (Latin for water of life). It seems we should be thankful to the good friars for more than just preserving the art of winemaking during the Dark Ages.

Q: What does the term "proof" mean on liquor bottles?

A: "Proof" expresses the proportion of alcohol in a beverage as twice the percent. For example, the standard 80-proof beverage is 40% alcohol. It derives from early days when proof of a whiskey used in barter was to mix it with gunpowder to see if it contained enough alcohol to burn. Whiskey had another indirect reference to gunpowder during the Civil War when President Lincoln was informed that General Grant drank whiskey while leading his troops. He reportedly replied, "Find out the name of the brand so I can give it to my other generals." Wine bottles give the actual percentage of alcohol content (within 1 1/2 %) on their labels as opposed to proof. Evidently wine does not mix well with gunpowder.

Q: I have been told the best place to keep my wine is in the refrigerator. Is that so?

A: It is, if you have opened a bottle and wish to save the remaining wine for a couple of days. Refrigeration will slow down the natural deterioration process after the wine has been exposed to oxygen. It will not keep much longer than a few days, however, so be sure to consume what is left within a couple days. Refrigeration of unopened bottles of wine should also be limited, even though they will keep for a longer period of time. The refrigerator is a popular hiding place for Champagne and other sparkling wine, but it is not the best place for storing your collection. Months of refrigeration will have a negative effect on the quality of all wines since the refrigerator is also a dehumidifier and it will eventually dry out the corks as well as vibrate the bottles every time the motor goes on and off. The optimum storage conditions are around a constant 55-60°F, free of light exposure and vibrations.

Q: Don't all wines keep getting better in the bottle as they get older?

A: Over 95% of the wines produced worldwide are meant to be consumed by the third year after their harvest. Only super premium red wines will continue to improve in the bottle for any length of time. It is also recommended to consume sparkling wines with plastic cork stoppers within a year's time, since CO_2 gases will leak out around the plastic corks and leave the wine flat. The best advice is not to save wine beyond a year or two unless you know that the wine you are saving is one that will improve over time. Your wine merchant or the originating winery will be your best advisor in this case.

Q: What is an appellation on a wine label and what does it guarantee the consumer?

A: Appellations are government designated viticultural regions that possess unique growing conditions and elements. The only guarantee you have is that at least 85% of the grapes used to make the wine are from that specific area. There is no guarantee of quality, although some appellations have a reputation for better performance than do others. Napa Valley certainly fits into that category.

Q: What does the term "Reserve" on a wine label mean?

A: In Italy and Spain the terms *Reserva* or *Riserva* have a very specific and legal meaning. In these countries the term is applied to wines that have been aged longer than the rest of the wines from that vintage. Wine producers traditionally apply the term only to the top quality wines that have been given special treatment and care. In the United States, label designations like Winemaker's Reserve and Vintage Select also have become a sign of special quality wines. Unlike Europe, however, there are no specific legal guidelines and a few United States producers will use the terminology as a marketing tool. A good test of reliability is to remember that special care and handling is involved in the making of these wines. They are not inexpensive to produce, so you will not likely find a true reserve for $4.99.

Q: Which United States president was noted as a wine connoisseur?

A: Thomas Jefferson developed an insatiable thirst for French wine during his five years serving as United States Minister to France. During his two-term presidency, Jefferson purchased over 20,000 bottles. He also experimented with vineyards on the property of his beloved Monticello. Today, there is a winery named Jefferson Vineyards in Jefferson's home state of Virginia.

Q: Where did the grape variety Syrah originate?

A: Legend has it that the Syrah grape came from the Persian city of Shiraz (the name of the grape as it known in Australia) and was introduced in France from Cyprus by Crusaders returning home from the Middle East in the 13th century. Also popular is the tale that Roman legions brought the grape variety from Egypt, via Syracuse. French winemakers, however, believe the grape variety is indigenous to France. Recent DNA research supports the French claim. It seems the parents of Syrah are Modeuse Blanche and Dureza, two lesser known French varieties that nature happened to cross pollinate to create a new genetic variety currently catching the fancy of wine consumers.

Q: How long has the Cabernet Sauvignon wine grape existed?

A: As popular as Cabernet Sauvignon has been for hundreds of years in Europe and now in the United States, one would be inclined to think that it is an indigenous variety. In fact, recent DNA research claims that Cabernet Sauvignon is the off-spring of a cross between Cabernet Franc and Sauvignon Blanc — a white grape, no less — and originated in the area of the Caspian Sea. By the way, the grape variety known as Cabernet Sauvignon accounts for only about 1 percent of the world's acreage planted to grapes.

Q: Are all oversized wine bottles given biblical names?

A: Other than the magnum, which literally means great or large, all oversize bottle sizes are named after biblical kings. The only exception to this rule is the Methusaleh, which takes its name from the longest-lived man in the Old Testament.

Jeroboam (Hebrew meaning "may the people multiply"): The first king of Israel. (I Kings 11:26)

Rehoboam (Hebrew meaning "enlarger of the people"): The son of Solomon by the Ammonite princess, Naamah. The first king of Judah. (I Kings 14:21,31)

Methuselah (Hebrew meaning "man of the dart"): The grandfather of Noah, and longest lived person in the Bible. He died at 969 years of age. (Genesis 5:21-27)

Salmanazar or *Shalmaneser* (Assyrian meaning "the god Sulman is chief"): The name of several Assyrian kings during the biblical period. (I Kings 16; II Kings 8; 10; 17)

Balthazar or *Belshazzar* (Babylonian meaning "the god Bel has protected the king"): Descendent of Nebuchadnezzar and co-regent with Nabonidus at the time Babylonia was conquered by Darius the Mede in 539 B.C. (Daniel 5:30; 7:1) One of the Magi has traditionally been known by this name also.

Nebuchadnezzar (Babylonian meaning "O Nabu, preserve the offspring"): Babylonian king who ruled from 605 to 562 B.C. (II Kings 24:7; 25:7)

Q: Is it true that early settlers in America were obligated to plant grape vines by law?

A: In 1623 the Virginia Colonial Assembly decreed that each household was required to plant a minimum of ten grape vines on their land. That is one way to assure a steady flow of wine in the state. As long as we are on the subject of Colonial America, here is an interesting bit of information:

Allegedly, the bill for a celebration party for the 55 drafters of the United States Constitution contained an order for 54 bottles of Madeira, 60 bottles of claret, 8 bottles of whiskey, 22 bottles of port, 8 bottles of hard cider, 12 beers and seven bowls of alcohol punch large enough that "ducks could swim in them."

Q: What wine was made famous by 14th century popes?

A: I believe you are referring to Chateauneuf-du-Pape (New Castle of the Pope), a famous wine of the Cotes du Rhone region of France. In 1309 a French pope moved the Papacy from Rome to Avignon in France. For the next sixty-eight years French Popes propagated new vineyards around their summer estates up river from their permanent residence in Avignon. The little summer getaway spot was called Chateauneuf-du-Pape. Only ruins remain of the castle, but the vineyards still produce a popular, quality red wine.

Q: How did the phenomena of White Zinfandel come about?

A: Like many inventions — by mistake. In 1972 California's Sutter Home Winery's emphasis was on producing big red wines. Sutter Home was owned by the Trinchero family and Bob Trinchero was their young winemaker. Bob, in his effort to produce a more robust red Zinfandel wine, begin experimenting using a complex French winemaking method that calls for withholding some of the freshly crushed juice from the skins during fermentation. This technique produced more concentrated flavors and deeper color in the resulting wine. All was working perfectly until Bob realized he had accumulated a big supply of the wine that was held out. The leftover wine looked pink due to the lack of contact with the grape skins. He had to dispose of it somehow, but could not throw it away because it was perfectly good. In fact, it was quite fruity and fresh tasting with a little left over residual sugar from the grapes. He simply bottled the stuff and christened it White Zinfandel. The result is one of the most popular styles of wines in the industry.

Q: I have a bottle of Italian wine called *Lachrima Christie.* If I remember my high school Latin correctly, it means "Tears of Christ." Could you tell me something about it?

A: You remember correctly. Lachrima Christie is a very soft and somewhat dry wine (available in both red or white) grown on the slopes of Mount Vesuvius, near Naples. Because of its delicate nature, it does not travel well nor does aging improve its structure. The Italians claim that it is best drunk young and while viewing the Bay of Naples. As with many Italian wines, there is also a legend that goes with it. According to legend (storytelling is the Italians' unique form of marketing), Christ came back to this little "part of Paradise" and found that the devil had conquered the inhabitants. In despair, the Lord sat on Mt. Vesuvius and wept. Where his tears fell there sprang up green vines. Obviously, the vines were of the Lachrima Christie vineyards and they have been popular ever since.

Q: I had a bottle of Italian wine called, "Est! Est! Est!" What kind of name is that for a wine?

A: It is Latin for "It is! It is! It is!" This light, semi-dry wine comes from an area around the village of Montefiascone, north of Rome. Legend has it that a German bishop on the way to a papal visit sent a servant ahead to check out the inns that served the best wines along his route. Wherever the wine was especially good, the servant was to write "Est" on the wall of the building as a mark of quality. Upon reaching Montefiascone, he wrote "Est! Est! Est!" The bishop never made it to Rome, and his tomb in this small village still stands as tribute to the indulging bishop's contribution to the economy of the area.

Q: On a recent trip to France we visited the Hospices de Beaune, a hospital run by charitable contributions and proceeds from their vineyard holdings. Do they actually make and sell wine to support the hospital?

A: The Hospices de Beaune was founded as a hospital for the sick, poor and aged residents of Beaune in 1443 by the Chancellor to the Duke of Burgundy. He endowed it with land in the Cote de Beaune for its continued income. Over the years other rich landowners have also bequeathed both vineyard and farmland to the hospital. At harvest time the crops are sold at public auction. For the wine, the third Sunday of November is auction day with enthusiastic wine merchants gathering from around the world. Traditionally, the prices achieved at the auction set the guideline for the selling of the rest of the wine of Burgundy that year. The profits from the auction do indeed support the continued management of the hospital, which now contains a wide assortment of modern medical equipment as well as historical works of art. The Hospices de Beaune also operates a popular museum and offers the public guided tours through the distinctive and beautiful architecture of the hospital and its grounds.

Q: Do you know who is attributed to saying, "My only regret in life is that I did not drink more Champagne?"

A: John Maynard Keynes, British economist who is considered a major architect in the creation of the economic structure of the United States of America, is credited with saying these words on his deathbed. To avoid life's regrets, take heed of these words from Benjamin Franklin, "Wine makes daily living easier, less hurried, with fewer tensions and more tolerance."

Q: What is the meaning of *en vino veritas*?

A: *En vino veritas* is Latin for "in wine is truth." That brings to mind the words of the French novelist, Colette: "Alone in the vegetable kingdom, the vine makes the true savor of the earth intelligible to man."

Q: Is it true that Marie Antoinette invented the Champagne glass?

A: French legend has it that Marie Antoinette was a big fan of the bubbly and that a creative glassmaker created the original shallow Champagne glass from wax molds made from Marie's breasts. The new sensual, glass goblet took France by storm. Ahh, those romantic French.

Q: Is it true that the German wine Liebfraumilch means "mother's milk?"

A: The popular wine of the Rhine is named after the original producer - the Librauenkirche (Church of the Holy Mother) near Worms. We have seen throughout history that the clergy of Europe played an important part in developing and preserving the art of winemaking. In this case, the famous blended wine received the name of Liebfraumilch - "Milk of the Blessed Mother" from the local monks. One of the most famous producers of this generic wine was Blue Nun, which was one of the top-selling wines in America in the 1960s and 1970s.

Q: Where did the French region called Cotes d'Or get its name? Was gold once mined there?

A: The gold of this renowned grape-growing area of Burgundy refers to the golden slopes of Chardonnay and Pinot Noir vineyards as they appear in autumn. However, some believe the gold has a financial meaning, as in "slopes of gold" since the region has had a long history of strong revenue production. Yet others offer one other interpretation. The golden sloping vineyards face east, or Orient in French, hence, Cotes d'Orient which through generations got shortened to Cotes d'Or. Take your pick.

Q: Is it true that there is a wine made from Limburger cheese.

A: There is a red wine made from the Limburger (or Lemburger) grape grown prominently in the state of Washington and British Columbia, Canada. The wine is very pleasant and usually made dry to complement dining. It does not have the characteristics of Limburger cheese, although the name is taken from the same Belgium province (Limburg) famous for the origination of the highly odorous dairy product.

Q: What is the association between wine and the precious stone amethyst in Greek mythology?

A: Amethyst's origin resides with the god Dionysus (Bacchus) and the goddess Diana. Dionysus, the god of wine, was insulted by a mortal who had refused him acknowledgment. Enraged with anger, Dionysus vowed to unleash his fury upon all mortals who did not partake in his gifts of wine. He spotted a young maiden named Amethyst who was pure and unfamiliar with being intoxicated. The unsuspecting young virgin, who was on her way to pay homage to the goddess Diana, was detained by the wrathful god. Dionysus summoned two fiercely voracious tigers to devour the youth and sat back with his wine to watch. Amethyst cried out to Diana. When Diana saw what was about to transpire she quickly transformed the young mortal into a glimmering pure white stone (quartz) to protect her from the vicious wrath of Dionysus. Moved with pity Dionysus realized the ruthlessness of his actions and began to weep with sorrow. As the tears dripped into his goblet Dionysus collapsed and the tear-tainted wine ran out onto the stone from the tipped cup. The white stone then absorbed the color from the wine creating the stone now called amethyst.

Q: Do you have any quotes on the subject of wine?

A: Wine cheers the sad, revives the old, inspires the young, makes weariness forget its toil. —*Lord Byron*

There is no gladness without wine. —*Talmud*

A glass of wine is a great refreshment after a hard day's work. —*Beethoven*

Wine is at the head of all medicines; where wine is lacking, drugs are necessary. —*Talmud*

A meal without wine is like a day without sunshine. —*Brillat-Savarin*

I feast on wine and bread, and feasts they are. —*Michelangelo*

Wine is light, held together by water. —*Galileo*

God loves fermentation just as dearly as he loves vegetation. —*Ralph Waldo Emerson*

Wine is the intellectual part of a meal, meats are merely the material part. —*Alexandre Dumas*

Water separates the people of the world, wine unites them —*Anonymous*

Wine & Health

Wine was given by God, not that we might be
drunken, but that we might be sober.
It is the best medicine when it has
moderation to direct it.
Wine was given to restore
the body's weaknesses,
not to overturn the soul's strength.

ST. CHRYSOSTOM

•

Amen to that, Brother.
Now please pass the red wine.

JOE BORRELLO

Q: So much has been written on the overindulgence of alcohol, but isn't alcohol and particularly wine, healthful when consumed in moderation?

A: Doctors are one of the largest occupational groups that participate in wine and food societies and clubs in America. They also encourage the use of moderate wine consumption because of its rich source of nutrients and the role it plays as a natural tranquilizer. Scientists have known for years that wine contains rich deposits of vitamins, minerals and natural sugars that are often times beneficial to good health. Red wines have more of these elements due to the juice's longer contact with the grapes' skin, which add to the mix. Red wines are rich in B vitamins derived from the grape skins. Both red and white wines contain important amounts of iron and contain less calories than most people think. A bottle of red or white dry wine contains about 500 calories. This will vary according to the combination of sugar and alcohol. Wine is also rich in potassium, low in sodium and works toward lowering cholesterol levels. Wine has long been used to fortify weak blood and to help ease sleeping problems. According to Dr. Russell V. Lee, Clinical Professor of Medicine, Stanford University School of Medicine, "There is no doubt at all that the moderate use of wine while eating is the most effective tranquilizer known to medical man." The key, like anything else, is not to abuse a good thing with overindulgence. Enjoy wine responsibly and common sense will tell you not to drink and drive. But for one reason or another, approximately one-third of all Americans refrain from consuming beer, wine, liquor or any other alcoholic beverage.

Q: Are there any wines made sulfite free?

A: In winemaking, sulfites are added early in the winemaking process for both biological and chemical purposes. They inhibit detrimental bacteria and prevent oxidation of the wine. With technical advances in the handling of wine, most winemakers have cut back extensively on the addition of sulfites. However, some yeasts produce sulfites on their own, through the natural fermentation process. It is virtually impossible to find a grape wine with less than 10 parts per million; the minimum government standard requiring a federal warning label. Fortunately, the vast majority of us are not affected by the small amounts normally found in wine and other foods.

Q: I understand virtually every wine contains sulfites, but what percentage of the population is actually sensitive to sulfites?

A: The human body naturally produces each day about the same amount of sulfites that are in one hundred bottles of wine. Only about one quarter of one percent of the United States population is allergic to sulfites and those people are usually well aware of their sensitivity.

Q: Which wines have the least amount of tannin?

A: Tannins are natural enzymes that help the wine age. Most all wines have some tannin, which is extracted from the grape skins and through barrel aging. However, red wines generally contain the most tannin residual because they usually have longer contact with the skins and wooden barrels during the winemaking procedure.

Q: Why does wine aid digestion?

A: According to some medical practitioners, the acidity in wine helps break down protein in the digestive process. As we pass the age of 50, it seems our system does not produce as much hydrochloric acid to aid digestion and hence, many doctors are suggesting a glass or two of wine with a meal. Wine also has a tranquil effect on the body and helps some people who have trouble sleeping. As St. Paul, the Apostle, said in 1 Timothy 5:23, "Drink no longer water, but use a little wine for thy stomach's sake." As in all consumption and responsible use of alcoholic beverages, moderation is the key to safe and healthful enjoyment.

Q: Does wine benefit the heart and circulatory system?

A: Through research there is now a worldwide consensus that moderate wine and alcohol consumption is associated with a reduced risk for coronary heart disease. "Numerous well-designed studies have concluded that moderate drinking is associated with improved cardiovascular health," wrote the director of the National Institute on Alcohol Abuse and Alcoholism (NIAAA), the United States government alcohol research agency, in 1996. According to a 1996 report from the American College of Cardiology, moderate drinkers "have a 40 percent to 50 percent reduction in coronary artery disease risk compared with individuals who are abstinent." Several studies have provided evidence that wine and alcohol are likely to benefit the cardiovascular system by raising the level of HDL cholesterol, lowering the level of LDL cholesterol and inhibiting the clotting of blood platelets.

Q: Are the health benefits of drinking hard liquor the same as wine?

A: If you drink hard liquor and want to live longer, switch to wine, a Danish study suggests. The ten-year study of 13,285 men and women, aged 30 to 70, found that people who drank wine regularly lived longer than those who abstained. The study showed significant results at the one or two glasses of wine per day level, but even greater benefits were derived at three to five glasses per day. Interestingly, hard liquor drinkers were shown to have increased their risk of dying (for any reason) by 30% over teetotalers, and beer drinkers did not benefit significantly. The findings were published in the *British Medical Journal.* "They've demonstrated that mortality decreased in proportion per glass of wine up to five glasses," said Irwin Wolkoff, a Canadian physician who writes a wine column for *The Medical Post,* in an interview with Associated Press. Morton Gronbaek of the Danish Epidemiology Science Center also attributes a 30% overall decline in coronary heart disease mortality in Denmark in the past 15 years to the dramatic increase in wine consumption since the opening of the European market made wine more affordable there. Dr. Wolkoff warned, however, that the risk for hemorrhagic strokes becomes greater with more than five glasses of wine a day. "The key is not to drink yourself silly."

Q: How many calories are in a glass of wine?

A: Calories come from the amount of alcohol and what is called residual sugar, which is left in the wine after the fermentation process. In general, a 5 ounce glass of wine will contain about a 100 calories. Given this information, wines that are sweeter or are fortified with alcohol (like Port and Sherries) will have as much as double the calories. These wines, however, are usually served in smaller quantities.

Q: How much of wine is water?

A: Wine is made up of approximately 80 to 85% water, 7 to 14% alcohol, 0 to 10% residual sugar, 1% natural acids and 1/2 to 1 % extract flavor components. These percentages fluctuate between styles and varieties of wine to add up to 100% pure pleasure.

Q: Why does red wine, but not white wine, cause headaches in some people?

A: Some wine researchers say that people have been getting headaches from red wine since Biblical times. Evidence has shown that the problem is not a hangover, since sufferers complain of pain after as little as a few sips of red wine. Nor is alcohol itself the culprit, since white wine does not affect people who suffer from RWH (Red Wine Headache — yes, it is an actual medical research term).

Initial theories suggested headaches might be due to a sensitivity to sulfites, preservatives added during the grape crush and fermentation, but white wine usually contains more residual sulfites. According to Herbert Kaufman, M.D., of the American Wine Alliance for Research and Education, studies suggest the prophylactic ingestion of aspirin prevented the red wine headache syndrome. In the studies, subjects with a history of RWH were tested with red wine, and all experienced headaches. One week later the volunteers were given either a placebo, a dose of aspirin or acetaminophen one hour before the ingestion of red wine. Those that took the placebo experienced the headache as usual, while the acetaminophen delayed the RWH syndrome for 6-10 hours. The subjects that took the aspirin, however, did not suffer any RWH effects. The findings suggest the headaches are caused by a hormonal-like chemical called *prostaglandin*, which is evidently curtailed by aspirin. The study does not reveal what in red wine triggers the release of prostaglandin, but they do know that the chemical can dilate blood vessels and turn up the sensitivity of pain receptors. Although aspirin ingested prior to the consumption of red wine may ward off the RWH syndrome, test results also verified that once RWH begins, aspirin had little or no effect in altering the headache.

Q: I have read that wine has been around since the beginning of civilization. What sort of evidence substantiates this claim?

A: A pottery jar found in the northern Zagros Mountains of Iran dates the earliest evidence of wine to between 5400 and 5000 B.C. The fermentation, use and preservation of wine, according to this archaeological discovery, have been part of human culture for at least 7000 years. "The new evidence belongs to the period when the first permanent human settlements, based on plant and animal domesticates and minor crafts such as pottery-making, were being established," wrote archaeologist and scientist Patrick McGovern and his colleagues, in the scientific journal *Nature*.

Recovered from a square mud brick building at the site of Hajji Firuz Tepe, Iran, the jar provides the earliest chemical evidence of wine to date, two millennia earlier than previous analysis indicated. Wine was identified by the presence of the calcium salt of tartaric acid, which occurs in large amounts only in grapes, and resin from the terebinth tree, which grows abundantly throughout the Near East.

According to the researchers, the new evidence "has important implications for the origins of viticulture as well as for the development of our modern diet, medical practice and society in general." The link between wine and health is apparent from the presence of terebinth resin, which was widely used in ancient times as an additive to wine to inhibit the growth of bacteria. Until early in the twentieth century, wine was universally used as a base for medicinal preparations compounded with various herbs tailored to specific ailments.

The article in *Nature* is the latest development stemming from a 1991 Northern California symposium, "The Origins and Ancient History of Wine." It was then that McGovern, an archaeologist with the University of Pennsylvania Museum, first announced the discovery of the long-necked jar with its substantial tartaric acid residue. At that time, the researchers had dated the jar to 3500 B.C., about 3000 years earlier than previous chemical evidence for wine. Subsequent laboratory analysis by McGovern, working with chemists Donald Glusker and Lawrence Exner along with archaeologist Mary Voigt, who originally excavated the relic, has now dated the origin of the jar to at least 5000 B.C. While wild grape seeds have been identified as far back as the 8th century B.C., this discovery marks the earliest scientific record of fermented wine as used by humans.

The ancient practice of including antibacterial elements in wine serves as a precursor to research going on today, as a recent study has found wine to be a powerful antibacterial agent. In a study led by University of West Virginia researcher Dr. Martin Weisse, wine was found to be more effective than even *bismuth salicylate* (the active ingredient in *Pepto Bismol*) in fighting bacteria responsible for food poisoning, dysentery and diarrhea. Ancient writings have long attested to the benefits of wine consumption, and this groundbreaking discovery provides more insight in the history and use of wine. As McGovern and colleagues explain, "Wine was a highly desirable grape product because of its unique dietary and medical benefits."

He causeth the grass to grow for the cattle, and herb for the service of man; that he may bring forth food out of the earth; and wine that maketh glad the heart of man.

(Psalm 104:14)

INDEX